STRENGTHEN YOUR CHILD'S BOND

Strengthen Your Child's Bond

Harper Greene

Contents

1

Dedication

Strengthening Your Child's Bond: A Guide to Understanding and Connecting

This book is dedicated to every parent who embarks on the incredible journey of raising a child. It's a journey filled with laughter, tears, challenges, and triumphs, a tapestry woven with threads of love, patience, and unwavering commitment.

This is for the parents who tirelessly strive to understand their children's unique emotional landscapes, who navigate the complexities of communication with grace and empathy, and who dedicate themselves to fostering strong, healthy, and lasting bonds. To those parents who seek knowledge, understanding, and practical tools to enhance their parenting skills and create a loving, supportive environment for their children to flourish – this book is for you. It is a testament to your dedication, your resilience, and your profound love. May it serve as a compass guiding you on this extraordinary adventure, empowering you to build a relationship with your child that is as strong, nurturing, and deeply fulfilling as the love you share. To all parents who seek to build a legacy of love and understanding, may this book provide the guidance you need. May it also provide comfort, encouragement, and a renewed sense of purpose. For those parents who have stumbled or are struggling, remember that your efforts matter and that every moment of connection is a step toward creating a lasting bond.

2

Preface

I've spent years witnessing the profound impact of parent-child relationships on a child's development and overall well-being. I've also had the privilege of witnessing the transformative power of strong, healthy bonds, where
children thrive, feel safe, understood, and empowered to reach their full potential. But I've also encountered parents who, despite their best intentions, struggle with the
complexities of parenting. The challenges are real: tantrums, meltdowns, difficult conversations, and the ever-present pressure to do it "right."

This book isn't about providing a perfect parenting formula; no such thing exists. Instead, it's about equipping you with the tools and insights needed to navigate the ups and downs of parenthood with confidence, compassion, and
understanding. It's about fostering a genuine connection with your child, built on a foundation of empathy, respect, and open communication.

This is not just a guide; it's an invitation to go on a journey of self-discovery as a parent, to learn and grow alongside your child, and to cultivate a relationship that will enrich both your lives for years to come.

My hope is that this book will serve as a reliable companion, offering practical strategies, relatable examples, and a

supportive voice to help you build the strongest, most loving connection with your child. It is a journey that is both
challenging and deeply rewarding, and I am honored to be a part of it. Let's endive on this adventure together.

3

Introduction

The relationship between a parent and child is perhaps the most fundamental and influential bond in a person's life. It shapes a child's emotional development, sense of security, and self-esteem, laying the foundation for their future relationships and overall well-being.

This book recognizes the profound importance of this bond and offers a comprehensive guide to building and nurturing a strong, healthy, and loving connection with your child. We'll explore the multifaceted nature of parent-child interactions, delving into the intricacies of emotional communication, active listening, and the art of validation.

We'll navigate the complexities of different developmental stages, offering tailored approaches to address the unique emotional needs of children at each age. We will address common parenting challenges, providing practical strategies and tools to manage conflict, set healthy boundaries, and navigate difficult conversations with empathy and grace.

This isn't a manual filled with rigid rules, but rather a supportive roadmap, designed to empower you with the knowledge and skills to build a strong parent-child bond that is deeply fulfilling and transformative.

This book will use real-life examples, relatable anecdotes, and a conversational tone, weaving together principles of child psychology with practical, actionable advice that you can immediately integrate into your parenting journey. We'll emphasize the importance of creating a safe, supportive, and emotionally enriching environment where your child feels seen, heard, and understood.

It's a journey that requires patience, understanding, and a willingness to grow and learn alongside your child. But the rewards – a deep and loving connection, a confident and resilient child, and a family built on mutual respect and understanding – are immeasurable. Let's begin this
rewarding journey together.

4

Recognizing Emotional Signals

Decoding a child's emotional landscape can feel like navigating a complex, ever-shifting terrain. One minute, your child is basking in the sunshine of joy, building magnificent Lego castles, the next they're engulfed in a tempest of tears, their small body trembling with frustration.

Understanding these emotional shifts, learning to read the subtle cues and decipher the underlying message, is a cornerstone of effective parenting. It's not about silencing the storm, but rather understanding the weather patterns.

This isn't about magically transforming your child into an emotionally placid being – that's not realistic or even desirable. It's about equipping them, and yourselves, with the tools to navigate the emotional weather with grace and understanding.

Children, unlike adults, often lack the sophisticated vocabulary to articulate their inner turmoil. Their emotional expressions are primarily conveyed through nonverbal cues: subtle shifts in posture, fleeting facial expressions, and the almost imperceptible tremor in their voice. A clenched jaw might betray simmering anger, while downcast eyes and a slumped posture could signal sadness or defeat. A child clutching a beloved toy might be seeking comfort during a moment of fear or insecurity. These nonverbal signals are the silent language of childhood, often more revealing than words.

Consider the difference between a two-year-old's frustrated wail after a tower of blocks collapses, and the same child's quiet whimper after a fall. The first is often a tantrum, fueled by frustration and a limited ability to self-regulate. The second might be a genuine expression of physical pain and

fear. Learning to discern these nuances is key. The tantrum might warrant a firm but empathetic response –
acknowledging the frustration without rewarding the
behavior. The whimper, however, demands comfort, a reassuring touch, and perhaps a gentle kiss to soothe the hurt.

The ability to decipher these cues becomes even more
crucial as children grow. A withdrawn preteen might be grappling with feelings of loneliness or anxiety, expressing it not through an outburst, but through a quiet retreat into their room or a marked decrease in interaction with friends and family. A pre-teen's silent struggle is quite different from the vocalized exasperation of a toddler. Understanding the
specific expressions for each age group is essential for
providing appropriate support.

The teenage years are a rollercoaster of emotional upheaval.

Hormonal shifts, social pressures, and the quest for
independence create a volatile mix. Teenage emotions might be expressed through sarcasm, eye-rolling, sullen silence, or even aggressive outbursts. Recognizing these as expressions of underlying anxieties, fears, or insecurities is critical. It's not about condoning the behavior; rather, it's about
understanding the emotional source. A slammed door might not just be defiance, but a desperate cry for understanding and connection.

Consider the following scenario: A six-year-old bursts into tears because their favorite crayon broke. An ineffective response would be: "Don't be silly, it's just a crayon." This dismisses the child's feelings and undermines their emotional experience. A more effective response would acknowledge their feelings: "Oh no, your favorite crayon broke. That must be really upsetting. It's okay to feel sad when something you love is broken." This validation doesn't negate the reality that

it's "just a crayon," but it acknowledges the genuine emotional impact on the child.

The subtle differences in facial expressions across ages also play a crucial role. A young infant's distress might manifest as a furrowed brow, tightly closed lips, and a pained cry. An older child might show their displeasure through a scowl, clenched fists, and a defiant posture. An adolescent might express their anger with a sarcastic remark or a dismissive wave of the hand. Each age has its own unique vocabulary of emotional expression. Learning to read these signals is akin to learning a new language, one that requires close observation, patience, and a willingness to understand from their perspective.

Vocal cues also offer valuable insights. The high-pitched wail of a frightened toddler contrasts sharply with the quiet sob of a heartbroken older child. The angry shouts of a frustrated teen are different from the controlled anger of a young adult. The tone, volume, and rhythm of a child's voice can reveal a great deal about their emotional state. This extends beyond merely the words being spoken. A child may say "I'm fine," but the trembling voice and downcast eyes may tell a different story. Trusting the non-verbal cues, often over the spoken words, especially in younger children, is vital.

Furthermore, cultural factors can influence how children express their emotions. Some cultures encourage open displays of affection and emotion, while others favor more reserved expressions. Recognizing these cultural norms will allow parents to interpret their child's emotional cues within the context of their background. A child from a culture that values stoicism might not express their emotions as openly as a child from a culture that celebrates exuberant emotional expression. However, the underlying emotional states are

still present, even if their outward manifestations differ. This highlights the need for cultural sensitivity in interpreting emotional cues.

Beyond the specific nonverbal cues, the context of the situation is crucial. A child who is usually outgoing and cheerful suddenly becomes withdrawn and quiet might be experiencing underlying stress or anxiety. This change in behavior, outside their typical emotional baseline, is a significant indicator that something might be wrong.

Therefore, understanding your child's emotional signals requires a holistic approach. It involves observing their nonverbal cues, listening attentively to their verbal

expressions (or lack thereof), considering the context of the situation, and acknowledging the influence of cultural

factors. By combining these elements, parents can develop a deeper understanding of their child's emotional world,

building a strong foundation of empathy, understanding, and connection. This, in turn, fosters a safe and supportive

environment where children feel comfortable expressing themselves, leading to healthier emotional development and a stronger parent-child bond. The journey of deciphering your child's emotional language is a lifelong process, one that requires patience, sensitivity, and an unwavering

commitment to understanding the unique individual before you. The rewards, however, are immeasurable.

5

Walking in Your Childs Shoes

Empathy. The word itself feels soft, almost gentle, yet its power in parenting is seismic. It's the bridge that spans the chasm between adult logic and a child's often bewildering emotional landscape. It's the key that unlocks
communication, fostering trust and understanding where frustration and conflict might otherwise reign. Without empathy, parenting becomes a power struggle, a battle of wills where the child's needs are often overlooked,
misinterpreted, or dismissed. With empathy, parenting
transforms into a collaborative journey, a shared exploration of emotions and experiences.

Think back to your own childhood. Remember a time when you felt truly understood, when someone saw beyond your tears or your tantrums to the core of your emotion? That feeling, that profound sense of validation, is the essence of what we aim to offer our children. It's not about agreeing with everything they do or say—far from it. It's about acknowledging their feelings, validating their experiences, and showing them that their emotions, however intense or seemingly illogical, are legitimate and worthy of attention.

Let's consider a common scenario: sibling rivalry. Imagine two children, Sarah and Tom, arguing over a toy. Without empathy, the

parental response might be swift and decisive:"Stop fighting! Share the toy!" This approach, while well-intentioned, fails to address the underlying emotions. Sarah might be feeling anger and frustration at having her
possession taken; Tom might feel triumphant and defensive. An empathetic response would begin with acknowledging each child's perspective. "Sarah, I see you're upset that Tom took your toy. That must be frustrating." Then, turning to

Tom: "Tom, I see you wanted to play with the toy too. But Sarah was playing with it first." This acknowledgment allows each child to feel heard, a crucial first step in de-escalating the conflict.

The empathetic approach goes further than simple acknowledgment. It requires us to step into our child's shoes, to imagine the world from their point of view. Consider a child's fear of the dark. To an adult, the darkness might seem harmless, just the absence of light. But to a child, the dark is a mysterious realm teeming with unknown creatures and potential dangers. Their fear isn't irrational; it's a product of their limited experience and developing imagination. An empathetic parent wouldn't dismiss the fear with a
dismissive "There's nothing to be afraid of!" Instead, they might validate the feeling: "It's okay to be scared of the dark. Lots of kids feel that way. Maybe we can leave a nightlight on, or I can sit with you until you fall asleep."

This approach, however, requires introspection and self-awareness on the parent's part. We must first be willing to examine our own emotional responses and recognize any potential biases or judgments. Are we projecting our own adult anxieties onto our child's fears? Are we judging their emotional reactions based on our own expectations of how they "should" behave? Honest self-reflection is paramount to developing effective empathy. Only by understanding our own emotional landscape can we truly appreciate and
navigate the emotional world of our children.

This process isn't always easy. Sometimes, our children's emotions trigger our own unresolved issues or past traumas.

A child's tantrum might trigger feelings of inadequacy or frustration within us. It's in these moments that self-compassion is crucial. We need to acknowledge that being a parent is challenging, that it's perfectly okay to feel overwhelmed or frustrated at times. Seeking support from a partner, family member, friend, or therapist can be invaluable during these periods.

Developing empathy is a journey, not a destination. It requires consistent practice and mindful attention. It's a skill that grows and evolves along with our children, adapting to their changing emotional needs. Here are some practical exercises that can help cultivate empathy in your parenting:

Active Listening:
Truly listen to your child without interrupting or judging. Focus on understanding their message, both verbal and nonverbal. Reflect back what you hear to ensure understanding. For example, instead of saying, "You shouldn't be so upset about losing that game,"try, "It sounds like you're really disappointed about losing the game. That must be hard."

Perspective-Taking:
Regularly ask your child about their feelings and perspectives. Inquire about their thoughts and feelings in specific situations. For instance, after a disagreement with a friend, ask, "Can you tell me what happened and how you felt about it?" Encourage them to articulate their emotional experience.

Mindful Observation:
Pay close attention to your child's nonverbal cues: body language, facial expressions, tone of voice. These cues often reveal more than words alone. A slumped posture and downcast eyes might indicate

sadness or disappointment, even if your child isn't explicitly stating these feelings.

Emotional Labeling:

Help your child identify and label their emotions. Provide them with vocabulary to express their feelings. For instance, if your child is crying, you might say, "It looks like you're feeling sad and frustrated right

now." This helps them develop emotional literacy and self-awareness.

Role-Playing:

Engage in role-playing scenarios where you take on the perspective of your child. This helps you better understand their experience and develop more empathetic responses. Imagine a situation where your child is being teased at school. Role-play the scenario with your child, taking on the role of the teaser and then the child who is being teased. This exercise can foster greater understanding and compassion.

Reading Literature:

Share books and stories with your child that explore a wide range of emotions and experiences. Discuss the characters' feelings and motivations. This helps children develop empathy for others and recognize the

complexity of human emotions.

Remember, empathy is not about condoning inappropriate behavior; it's about understanding the underlying reasons behind that behavior. A child who is hitting might be

expressing anger or frustration that they haven't yet learned to manage effectively. An empathetic response wouldn't simply be to punish the child, but to help them identify and regulate their emotions. It's a process of teaching and

guiding, of helping the child learn healthier coping

mechanisms.

Building empathy within the parent-child relationship is an ongoing process. It's about creating a space where

vulnerability is welcomed, where feelings are not judged but ac-

knowledged, and where a child feels safe to express their entire emotional spectrum, without fear of rejection or
dismissal. The rewards far outweigh the effort: a stronger, healthier relationship, a more emotionally resilient child, and a deeper understanding of the incredible, complex, and often

baffling world of childhood. In essence, it's about building a bridge of understanding, one heartfelt connection at a time. And that is a journey worth undertaking.

6

____

Truly Hearing Your Childs Voice

Active listening isn't merely about hearing the words your child speaks; it's about truly understanding the emotions behind them, the unspoken anxieties, the budding hopes, the simmering frustrations. It's about stepping into their world, even if for a brief moment, and seeing it through their eyes.

Imagine a small child, tears streaming down their face, clutching a broken toy. The immediate parental reaction might be to offer a solution: "Don't worry, we can get you a new one!" But this misses the point entirely. The child isn't just grieving a toy; they're grieving a connection, a sense of security, a part of their world that has suddenly fractured.

Active listening begins by acknowledging that loss, that feeling.

Effective active listening involves a conscious effort to set aside your own agenda, your own worries, your own
immediate solutions. It requires a shift in focus, a turning inward toward your child's emotional state. This isn't about passive agreement; it's about genuine understanding and empathy. It's about creating a safe space where your child feels heard, valued, and respected, regardless of the content of their message. This safe space allows for vulnerability, for the expression of feelings that may be messy, illogical, or

15

even frightening to the adult mind. Think of it as building a bridge of understanding, one empathetic response at a time.

Consider this scenario: a teenager comes home visibly upset after a disagreement with a friend. The knee-jerk reaction might be to offer advice: "You should have just..." or "You know, maybe they're right..." But this, in most cases, will only escalate the situation. Instead, try active listening. Begin by acknowledging their feelings: "Wow, you seem

really upset. Can you tell me what happened?" Then, listen intently. Avoid interrupting, even if their narrative seems rambling or illogical. Your role isn't to judge or correct; it's to listen, to understand, and to validate their emotions.

Active listening also involves reflecting back what your child has said, not to parrot their words, but to demonstrate your understanding. For instance, if your child says, "I hate school! Everyone is mean to me," you could respond with, "It sounds like you're feeling really hurt and lonely at school right now. That must be really tough." This demonstrates that you've heard them, that you understand their pain, and that you're willing to listen further. This isn't about fixing the problem immediately; it's about creating a connection, a sense of being understood, which is often the first step
towards finding solutions.

The power of reflecting back lies in its ability to validate the child's feelings. It shows that you are not only listening to their words but also paying attention to their emotional state.

Even if you don't fully understand their perspective,
reflecting their feelings allows them to feel heard and
understood, which in turn can help to de-escalate the
situation. Imagine a child complaining about an unfair rule at home. Instead of dismissing their concerns, try, "It sounds like you feel that the rule isn't fair and that's frustrating for you." This acknowledges their feelings without necessarily agreeing with their perspective. This simple act of

acknowledgement can go a long way in building trust and promoting open communication.

Let's contrast this with ineffective listening styles. Imagine the same scenario of the child complaining about the unfair rule. An ineffective response would be: "Oh, don't be silly; that rule is perfectly reasonable." This dismisses the child's feelings and invalidates their experience. Another ineffective

strategy is interrupting: "Let me tell you why the rule is there..." This again, demonstrates a lack of empathy and shows the child that their feelings are unimportant. Offering unsolicited advice before fully understanding the situation is also counterproductive. It sends a message that the child's feelings are less important than your solution.

The difference between active and passive listening is profound. Passive listening is essentially hearing the words without engaging emotionally or mentally. It's a surface-level interaction, lacking the depth and empathy that active listening provides. You might hear the words, but you're not truly present in the conversation. Your mind may be wandering, thinking about your to-do list, or planning your next response, instead of focusing entirely on your child.

Active listening requires mindfulness, a complete presence in the moment. It necessitates silencing your inner critic, letting go of your own assumptions and biases, and creating space for your child's experience. It's about understanding their perspective, even if you don't agree with it. This doesn't mean you have to condone every behavior or agree with every viewpoint; it means acknowledging and validating their feelings, showing them that their emotions are important, even if their actions aren't.

A crucial aspect of active listening is body language.

Maintain eye contact, nod to show that you are following along, and use open and inviting body posture. Avoid distractions like your phone or other tasks. Show your child that you are fully present and focused on them. Your

physical presence should reflect your commitment to
listening. A slumped posture or distracted gaze sends a message that you are not fully engaged, undermining the effectiveness of your listening.

Active listening isn't a skill acquired overnight. It takes practice, patience, and a genuine commitment to
understanding your child's perspective. It's a continuous learning process, requiring self-reflection and a willingness to adapt your approach to your child's unique needs and developmental stage. Sometimes, children may express themselves indirectly through their behavior. A child who is constantly misbehaving might be signaling underlying
emotional distress. In such cases, active listening involves observing their behavior, trying to understand the underlying emotions, and then creating an opportunity to discuss those feelings.

Consider a young child who is suddenly throwing tantrums. Instead of immediately reprimanding them, try to understand the root cause. Perhaps they are experiencing increased stress at school, are feeling overwhelmed, or are struggling to express themselves verbally. Active listening in this case would involve creating a safe space for them to express their emotions, even if it means sitting with them during a tantrum and providing comfort and reassurance.

Active listening extends beyond verbal communication. It includes observing your child's nonverbal cues: their facial expressions, body language, and tone of voice. These nonverbal cues often convey more than words can express.

A child who is fidgeting or avoiding eye contact might be feeling anxious or uncomfortable. Paying attention to these nonverbal signals allows you to better understand their emotional state and adjust your communication accordingly.

Building strong communication skills is an ongoing
investment in your relationship with your child. It's about creating a secure and supportive environment where your child feels comfort-

able expressing themselves without judgment or fear of reprimand. It's about building trust,

fostering empathy, and nurturing a bond that will last a lifetime. Through consistent practice of active listening, you'll not only improve your communication with your child but also strengthen your relationship and foster their

emotional well-being. Remember, it's not just about fixing problems; it's about being truly present for your child,

witnessing their growth, and sharing in their journey. The reward? A deeper, more meaningful connection with your child, built on mutual understanding and respect.

7

Affirming Your Childs Feelings

Understanding your child's emotional landscape is a journey of discovery, a continuous process of learning their unique language of feelings. We've explored the power of active listening, the art of truly hearing beyond the words to the underlying emotions. But hearing isn't enough; it's the
subsequent acknowledgement and validation of those
feelings that truly fosters emotional growth and a secure parent-child bond. Think of it as offering a safe harbor in the storm of a child's emotional experience.

Emotional validation is not about agreeing with every
behavior your child exhibits. A child might throw a tantrum because they didn't get the toy they wanted, and validating their feelings doesn't mean condoning the tantrum. Instead, it means acknowledging the intense frustration,
disappointment, or anger they are feeling. It's a powerful demonstration of empathy, a bridge built between your
understanding and your child's experience. It's about saying, "I see you, I hear you, and I understand what you're going through."

Let's illustrate this with some contrasting examples. Imagine your eight-year-old, Lily, comes home from school in tears because she wasn't chosen for the school play. An invalidating response might be, "Oh, don't be silly, there will be other chances. It's not a big deal." This dismisses Lily's feelings, implying her disappointment is trivial. It shuts down her emotional expression, leaving her feeling unheard and alone in her hurt. The emotional message she receives is, "My feelings aren't important."

A validating response, on the other hand, would acknowledge her hurt and disappointment. You might say, "Lily, I can see you're really upset about not getting a part in the play. That must be so disappointing after all the work you put into preparing." Notice the difference? This response doesn't minimize her feelings; it acknowledges their legitimacy. It validates her experience, making her feel seen and understood. It's a powerful message: "Your feelings are important, and it's okay to feel this way."

This difference, seemingly subtle, has profound long-term consequences. Children who consistently experience emotional validation develop a stronger sense of self-awareness, understanding their own emotions better. They learn to label their feelings accurately, differentiating between sadness, anger, frustration, and disappointment. This emotional literacy is crucial for healthy development.

They become better equipped to manage their emotional responses, developing coping mechanisms and resilience in the face of adversity.

Consider another scenario. Six-year-old Tom is furious because his brother, Mark, broke his favorite Lego castle. An invalidating response might be, "You're being too dramatic, it's just a toy. Boys don't cry." This not only dismisses his anger but also reinforces harmful gender stereotypes. It sends the message that expressing his emotions, particularly anger, is inappropriate and unacceptable.

A validating response might go something like this: "Tom, I can see how angry you are. It really hurts to have something special broken, especially something you worked hard on. It's okay to be angry.

Tell me more about how you feel." This response acknowledges his anger without condoning any potential aggressive actions directed at Mark. It opens the door for communication, allowing Tom to express his

feelings fully and safely. It also teaches him that his anger is a valid emotion, not something to be suppressed or ashamed of. This sets the stage for learning healthy conflict resolution skills.

Emotional validation is a continuous process, not a one-time fix. It requires consistent effort and a genuine desire to

understand your child's world. It demands patience and empathy, even during challenging moments. It's about

creating a safe space where your child feels comfortable expressing their full range of emotions, from joy and

excitement to sadness, anger, and fear. This safe space

fosters trust, making it easier for your child to turn to you for support during times of emotional distress. A parent who validates their child's feelings becomes a trusted confidante, an anchor in the storms of childhood.

The benefits extend far beyond the immediate situation.

Children who are emotionally validated are more likely to develop healthy self-esteem. They feel secure in their

identity, understanding that their emotions are valid and accepted. This sense of security translates into greater

resilience. When faced with challenges, they are better equipped to cope, knowing that their feelings are understood and supported. They are less likely to resort to unhealthy coping mechanisms like aggression, withdrawal, or self-harm.

Imagine a teenager dealing with the pressures of school, social situations, and the complexities of adolescence. A parent who consistently validated their emotions throughout childhood is likely to have a stronger, more trusting

relationship with their teenager. This allows for open

communication, allowing the teenager to seek guidance and support during these formative years. It builds a foundation of mutual respect and understanding that extends beyond

adolescence, strengthening the parent-child bond well into adulthood.

Furthermore, emotionally validating your child helps them develop stronger social skills. By witnessing you validating their emotions, they learn to empathize with the feelings of others. They learn the importance of understanding and acknowledging different perspectives, a crucial component of healthy relationships. This ability to understand and empathize with others will serve them well throughout their lives.

It is important to differentiate between validating feelings and validating behavior. Validating feelings means

acknowledging and accepting the emotions your child is experiencing. Validating behavior, on the other hand, means approving of their actions, even if they are inappropriate. These are two distinct concepts. You can validate a child's sadness about a lost opportunity without condoning any tantrum or aggressive behavior that might accompany it.

For example, a child might be upset about a friend betraying them. You can validate their feelings of hurt and betrayal by saying, "I understand you're feeling really hurt and betrayed by your friend. That's a very painful experience." This does not mean that you endorse any subsequent actions the child might take, such as spreading rumors about their friend or engaging in bullying behavior. Addressing the inappropriate behavior requires setting clear boundaries and explaining the consequences.

Let's consider the scenario of a child who consistently gets angry when things don't go their way. While you can validate their anger, "I know you're feeling really angry because you didn't get to play video games," you can simultaneously set a boundary, "However, it's not okay to throw your toys or yell at your brother when you're angry. We need to find healthier ways to express your anger."

This approach teaches the child that it's acceptable to feel angry but that there are appropriate and inappropriate ways to express those feelings. It fosters emotional regulation, a critical life skill that equips children to navigate their

emotions effectively throughout life. This careful balance between validating feelings and setting boundaries is

essential for raising emotionally intelligent and well-adjusted children. It is a key component in developing a strong and healthy parent-child relationship built on trust,

understanding, and mutual respect. It is an investment that yields substantial returns, strengthening the bonds of family and fostering a child's lifelong emotional well-being. The journey of understanding and validating your child's

emotional world is a rewarding one, a testament to the power of connection and empathy. The rewards extend far beyond childhood, shaping the very fabric of your relationship and fostering a lifetime of healthy emotional development for your child.

8

The Cornerstone of a Strong ParentChild Bond

Building trust is the bedrock upon which a strong and enduring parent-child relationship is built. It's more than just a feeling; it's the tangible manifestation of consistent reliability, empathy, and unconditional love. It's the knowing that even amidst disagreements or disappointments, the fundamental bond remains unbroken. This trust, meticulously cultivated, allows children to feel safe to explore their world, to take risks, to stumble and fall knowing that a supportive hand awaits their return. Without it, the emotional landscape becomes treacherous, filled with apprehension and fear, hindering a child's ability to thrive emotionally and socially.

Active listening, as we've discussed, is the first crucial step in building this trust. When a child feels heard—truly heard, not just passively listened to—they experience a profound sense of validation. This isn't simply about responding to their words, but also to the unspoken emotions underpinning them. A child's tearful complaint about a lost toy isn't just about the toy; it's about feeling lost, helpless, and perhaps even a tinge of disappointment in themselves. Recognizing and acknowledging these underlying feelings—the frustration, the sadness, the vulnerability—demonstrates empathy and understanding. This act of empathy is the cornerstone of trust. It conveys the message: "I see you, I hear you, and I understand."

Emotional validation goes hand-in-hand with active listening. It's about accepting a child's feelings without judgment, even if you don't agree with their behavior. Telling a child that their anger is valid, even if their response to that anger is inappropriate, helps them understand that their

feelings are legitimate. It doesn't mean condoning their actions; rather, it separates the feeling from the behavior, allowing for constructive guidance. For example, if a child throws a tantrum because they can't have a second cookie, acknowledging their frustration ("I know you're really

disappointed you can't have another cookie") while setting a clear boundary ("We agreed on one cookie, and it's important to stick to our agreements") allows the child to process their feelings without feeling dismissed or invalidated. This

consistency in your approach reinforces trust, teaching the child that your love and acceptance are unwavering even during challenging moments.

Keeping promises is another vital element in cultivating trust. It might seem simple, but the consistent fulfillment of even small promises, from reading a bedtime story to taking them to the park, builds a strong sense of reliability.

Breaking promises, even seemingly insignificant ones, can significantly erode a child's trust. If you say you'll be home by 6 pm, strive to be there. If you promise a trip to the zoo, make every effort to follow through. Understanding that actions speak louder than words, parents should ensure their promises are realistic and achievable. And if, unexpectedly, a promise cannot be kept, a sincere explanation and a revised plan is crucial. Honesty and transparency in these situations are paramount to rebuilding trust.

Consistency in your actions and boundaries is equally important. Children thrive on routine and predictability.

Consistent discipline, fair and firm, helps children understand expectations and limits, creating a sense of security. Inconsistent discipline, on the other hand, can be confusing and anxiety-inducing, making it difficult for a child to learn and trust established rules and boundaries. Imagine a child who is punished for touching a hot stove one day but not the next—the inconsistency breeds uncertainty

and undermines the parent's authority. This uncertainty erodes trust, making it harder for the child to learn self-regulation and to trust their parent's guidance.

Showing genuine care and affection is another crucial aspect of building trust. Physical affection, such as hugs, cuddles, and kisses, communicates love and security. But verbal affirmations are just as vital. Regularly telling your child that you love them, that you're proud of them, and that you appreciate them builds a strong emotional foundation. These affirmations aren't mere platitudes; they're powerful expressions of unconditional love. Expressing interest in their lives, asking about their day, and actively engaging in their hobbies and interests demonstrates genuine concern and strengthens the parent-child connection. This active engagement validates their individuality and nurtures their self-esteem. The time spent showing affection, though seemingly small, reinforces the message of unconditional love and security.

Sometimes, despite our best efforts, trust is broken. Perhaps a secret was revealed unintentionally, a promise was broken, or a boundary was crossed. Repairing this breach requires honesty, empathy, and a commitment to rebuilding the bond. Acknowledge the mistake, apologize sincerely, and explain why the breach occurred. Avoid making excuses or minimizing the impact of the action. Listening to the child's feelings without interruption is crucial. Let them express their hurt and anger without interruption. This listening helps the child feel heard and understood, reducing the underlying fear and resentment. The acknowledgment of their feelings lays the groundwork for a stronger, more resilient

relationship.

The process of rebuilding trust can take time and requires patience. It's a gradual restoration of faith, not a quick fix.

Consistent positive actions, showing reliability and

continuing to show empathy and genuine care, are essential steps in this process. Consistent displays of love, small gestures of affection, and fulfilling your commitments rebuild the child's confidence in your reliability. It may involve making amends, engaging in activities that foster connection and mutual understanding, and continuously demonstrating commitment to upholding trust. This slow, steady rebuilding process eventually leads to a deeper and more enduring bond, fortified by the experience of

overcoming a challenge together.

Building trust is a continuous process, a journey rather than a destination. It's a dynamic interaction requiring consistent effort and mindful attention. It's not about perfection; it's about striving to create a consistently safe and secure

environment where a child feels loved, respected, and

understood. It's about being present, attentive, and

responsive, ready to navigate the twists and turns of

childhood with patience, empathy, and a unwavering

commitment to nurturing a loving and trusting relationship. The effort invested in building a trustworthy relationship is an investment in the child's emotional well-being and the strength of the parent-child bond for years to come. This bond, fortified by mutual respect and understanding, will shape the child's life, providing a secure base from which they can explore the world, take risks, and ultimately, flourish. The journey of trust-building is a testament to the powerful, enduring nature of the parent-child relationship and its profound impact on a child's development.

Remember, the love and trust you cultivate will resonate far beyond the confines of childhood, shaping the very fabric of your relationship and fostering lifelong emotional well-being for both parent and child. This continuous process of
cultivating trust is a deeply rewarding aspect of parenthood,

providing a framework for a loving, lasting, and meaningful bond.

9

Responding to Early Emotional Needs

The first two years of a child's life are a whirlwind of incredible growth and development, a period laying the groundwork for their future emotional landscape. It's a time of profound vulnerability and dependence, where the parent-child bond becomes the cornerstone of their emotional
security. Understanding and responding to the unique
emotional needs of infants and toddlers is not just crucial for their immediate well-being; it profoundly shapes their ability to navigate the complexities of emotions throughout life.

Infancy is a symphony of nonverbal communication. Long before a baby can articulate their needs, they express
themselves through subtle cues – a furrowed brow signaling discomfort, a tight fist indicative of anxiety, a wide, gummy grin brimming with joy. Learning to decipher these
nonverbal signals is paramount. A cry, for instance, isn't simply a demand for attention; it's a complex
communication system conveying hunger, discomfort,
loneliness, or even simply the need for reassurance. Paying close attention to the nuances of the cry – its pitch, intensity, and rhythm – can help parents discern the underlying
emotion and respond appropriately. A high-pitched, piercing cry

might suggest pain or intense distress, demanding
immediate attention, while a low, rhythmic whimper might indicate tiredness or mild discomfort.

Responsive parenting, the bedrock of healthy emotional development during infancy, involves observing these subtle cues and responding promptly and consistently. This isn't about instantly fulfilling every whim; it's about providing a secure and predictable environment where the baby feels safe, understood, and loved. Consistent responses to a baby's

needs, particularly those related to comfort and security, foster a sense of trust and predictability, essential
components of a secure attachment. This early attachment acts as a secure base, enabling the child to explore their world confidently, knowing that they have a reliable haven to return to when feeling overwhelmed or insecure.

Soothing techniques are crucial in this responsive parenting approach. Skin-to-skin contact, the gentle rhythm of rocking or swaying, the soft hush of a lullaby – these simple yet powerful actions tap into the baby's innate need for physical closeness and comfort. The warmth and familiarity of the parent's touch provide a sense of safety and security, calming the nervous system and helping the baby regulate their
emotions. The benefits extend beyond immediate comfort; consistent soothing helps the baby develop self-soothing skills, a crucial ability in managing stress and emotional regulation later in life.

Meeting a baby's basic needs is non-negotiable. Hunger, thirst, cleanliness, and a comfortable temperature are
fundamental to their emotional well-being. Ignoring these needs can lead to frustration, distress, and a sense of
insecurity. Consistent and timely responses to these needs demonstrate to the baby that their needs are valued and that their caregiver is reliable. This predictability lays the
foundation for a secure attachment and reduces the

likelihood of developing anxiety or attachment issues. Think of it like building a sturdy house; the foundation (basic needs) must be strong to support the rest of the structure (emotional well-being).

Beyond the immediate needs, fostering a sense of security and comfort is paramount. Creating a predictable routine, such as consistent feeding and sleep schedules, provides a sense of structure and stability, easing anxiety and promoting

a feeling of safety. Familiar toys, comforting blankets, and consistent caregivers contribute to this sense of stability. A predictable environment enables the infant to develop a sense of self and confidence, knowing what to expect and reducing fear of the unknown.

The impact of early attachment on future emotional development cannot be overstated. Securely attached infants develop a positive self-image, better emotional regulation skills, and stronger relationships throughout life. They are better equipped to cope with stress, navigate challenging situations, and build healthy relationships with others.

Conversely, insecure attachment, often stemming from inconsistent or unresponsive parenting, can lead to various emotional challenges, including anxiety, depression, and difficulties forming healthy relationships later in life.

Let's consider some practical examples. Imagine a six-month-old who is crying inconsolably. A parent who understands the importance of responsive parenting might first assess the situation: Is the baby hungry? Wet?

Uncomfortable? If no immediate physical need is apparent, the parent might offer comfort through skin-to-skin contact, gentle rocking, or a soothing lullaby. They might whisper reassuring words, providing a sense of security and

connection. This consistent response helps the baby feel understood and loved, building a foundation of trust that will serve them well in their future emotional development.

In contrast, imagine a parent who dismisses the baby's cries, perhaps with statements like, "You're just being fussy," or "Stop crying, it's nothing." This response, while seemingly benign, can have a detrimental impact. The baby learns that their emotional needs are not valued, leading to potential feelings of insecurity and a weakening of the parent-child

bond. This can lead to difficulties in emotional regulation and challenges in forming secure attachments later in life.

The crucial takeaway is that responsiveness isn't about spoiling a child. It's about creating a foundation of trust, security, and emotional understanding that will empower the child to navigate the emotional landscape of their lives.

Meeting basic needs, providing consistent soothing, and understanding the nuances of nonverbal communication are all vital steps in nurturing a secure attachment and promoting healthy emotional development.

Moreover, the importance of creating a nurturing and stimulating environment cannot be overlooked. Engaging with the infant through playful interactions, providing opportunities for exploration, and offering a variety of sensory experiences contributes to their overall development and emotional well-being. Reading to a baby, singing songs, and playing games not only stimulates their cognitive development but also strengthens the bond between parent and child, providing a secure and loving context for emotional growth.

The period between 12 and 24 months marks a significant transition. Babies are becoming more mobile, independent, and increasingly aware of their emotions and the emotions of others. While the need for responsive care remains crucial, parents will now start to see the emergence of more complex emotions, such as frustration, anger, and jealousy. Tantrums may become more frequent, reflecting the child's growing frustration with limitations and their developing communication skills. This is a critical time to start fostering emotional self-regulation, encouraging the child to express their feelings appropriately and develop healthy coping mechanisms. Remember, patience and consistency are key.

The child is still learning to regulate their emotions, and a calm, understanding parent can be a crucial guide during these emotionally challenging moments.

Understanding the unique emotional needs of infants and toddlers is not just about providing for their physical requirements; it's about cultivating a strong and secure attachment that will serve as a bedrock for their emotional well-being throughout life. By being responsive, nurturing, and attentive to their nonverbal cues, parents can lay the foundation for a lifetime of healthy emotional development. The journey is not without challenges, but the rewards of a secure and loving parent-child bond are immeasurable. Every smile, every cuddle, every shared moment contributes to the rich tapestry of their emotional development, shaping their future capacity for love, resilience, and emotional intelligence. The early years are a time of profound shaping, and as parents, we hold the power to guide our children towards a path of healthy emotional growth.

10

Fostering Emotional SelfRegulation

Preschool years—ages three to five—mark a significant leap in a child's emotional development. While the foundational work of secure attachment laid in infancy continues to be crucial, this stage presents a new set of challenges and
opportunities for fostering emotional self-regulation. Think of it as building the scaffolding for a skyscraper; the
foundation is already there, but now we're adding the
complex framework that will support future growth. This stage isn't just about navigating tantrums (though those certainly play a prominent role!), it's about equipping your child with the tools to understand, manage, and express their emotions effectively. This process will shape their ability to form healthy relationships, cope with stress, and navigate the ups and downs of life with greater resilience.

One of the most striking changes in preschoolers is the
explosion of language. This newfound ability to articulate their inner world opens up incredible possibilities for
emotional understanding. However, it also means that their frustration, anger, and sadness can be expressed with a more forceful and articulate voice—often leading to what we often term "tantrums." These aren't simply attention-seeking
behaviors; they are genuine expressions of overwhelming emotions

that the child lacks the skills to process and
manage. Instead of viewing tantrums as acts of defiance, it's vital to
see them as cries for help, a sign that your child needs support in navigating their feelings.

Building an emotional vocabulary is a key strategy in
fostering self-regulation. Preschoolers are like sponges, absorbing the
language they hear around them. By enriching your child's vocabulary
with emotion words – "frustrated,"

"excited," "sad," "angry," "peaceful," "calm" – you provide them
with the labels they need to identify and understand what they are
feeling. You might say something like, "I see you're really frustrated
because you can't build the tower the way you want. It's okay to feel
frustrated." This validation of their feelings is key; it assures them that
their emotions are acceptable and don't need to be suppressed. Remember, naming the emotion doesn't dismiss it; it gives it a voice.

Modeling appropriate emotional expression is another
crucial step. Children learn by observing the adults in their lives. If
you consistently demonstrate healthy ways of
managing your own emotions, your child will learn to
emulate these behaviors. Imagine a situation where you are feeling
stressed; instead of lashing out or bottling up your feelings, you could
say aloud, "I'm feeling stressed right now because of work. I'm going
to take a few deep breaths and then call my friend to talk about it."
This shows your child a tangible example of how to manage challenging emotions, demonstrating self-soothing techniques and seeking support when needed. Make it a teachable moment. "See Mommy
is taking deep breaths because she's stressed? That helps calm me
down."

Remember, consistency is key. If you react differently to similar
situations at different times, your child will be
confused and struggle to learn effective coping mechanisms.

This is a process that involves repeated exposure and consistent reinforcement. Don't expect immediate results; it's a marathon, not a sprint.

Distraction techniques can be particularly effective with preschoolers, especially in the heat of the moment. When a tantrum is erupting, calmly and gently redirect their attention to another activity. This doesn't mean ignoring the feelings; it's about offering a temporary escape route from the

overwhelming emotion. "I see you're upset. Let's go play with your cars for a few minutes. We can come back to the blocks later." However, remember that simply distracting your child without addressing the underlying emotional cause might not be a sustainable solution in the long run. It's crucial to return to the original issue after they've calmed down, offering support and guidance.

Providing choices is another powerful tool. Giving a preschooler a sense of control can significantly reduce frustration and tantrums. Rather than saying, "It's time to clean up your toys," try "Do you want to clean up your blocks first or your cars?" Small choices can make a big difference in their sense of agency, empowering them to feel in control of their environment and reducing resistance.

However, it is equally important to set clear and consistent boundaries. While giving choices fosters autonomy, clear boundaries help children understand expectations and limits. For example, if hitting is unacceptable, clearly state this rule and consistently enforce it. "Hitting hurts other people, and we don't hit. If you're angry, you can tell me, and we can find another way to express your feelings."

Beyond tantrums, other emotional challenges arise during the preschool years. Jealousy among siblings, anxiety about separation from caregivers, or fear of the dark are all common occurrences. Address these emotions with empathy and understanding, validating your child's feelings without dismissing them. "It's okay to feel jealous when your sister gets a new toy. It's tough

when you feel like you're not
getting what you want." Offer reassurance and help your child develop coping mechanisms. For fear of the dark, a nightlight or a comforting bedtime routine can be immensely helpful.

Remember, fostering emotional self-regulation is a
collaborative process. It's a partnership between parent and child, where parents provide the guidance, tools, and
support, and the child learns to apply these skills in their own life. Don't be discouraged by setbacks. Preschoolers are still learning to navigate the complex landscape of emotions, and there will be times when they struggle. This is part of the process. By consistently modeling appropriate behavior, providing supportive feedback, and offering age-appropriate strategies, you'll equip your child with the emotional
resilience they need to thrive.

Empathy is the cornerstone of this journey. Try to see the world through your child's eyes. Understand that their emotional outbursts are often a reflection of their limited cognitive abilities and emotional processing skills. Their tantrums, meltdowns, and anxieties aren't personal attacks; they're expressions of their struggle to cope with the overwhelming emotions swirling inside. This empathy allows you to respond with patience, understanding, and a reassuring presence.

Furthermore, incorporating play therapy into your parenting approach can be incredibly beneficial. Preschoolers
communicate effectively through play. By engaging in imaginative play with your child, you can subtly address their emotional concerns and anxieties. For instance, if your child is struggling with separation anxiety, you can act out scenarios of leaving and returning, incorporating their
feelings and addressing their concerns through role-playing.

Play therapy allows for a safe and non-threatening space where emotions can be explored, processed, and ultimately resolved.

Storytelling can also be a powerful tool. Sharing stories about characters experiencing similar emotions helps

normalize their feelings and shows them that it's okay to feel a range of emotions, both positive and negative. Use books, cartoons, or even make up your own stories that depict

children dealing with everyday emotional challenges. This approach can help them process their own feelings indirectly, reducing the pressure of direct confrontation while offering a valuable learning experience. The storytelling can provide a space to explore possible solutions and develop coping

strategies within the safety of a fictional context.

Remember to celebrate your child's progress. Each time your child displays improved self-regulation, acknowledge their achievement. This positive reinforcement encourages them to continue practicing these skills. Instead of focusing solely on negative behaviors, highlight the positive moments. For example, if your child handled a frustrating situation without resorting to a tantrum, praise their effort and ability to

manage their emotions. This positive approach fosters a supportive environment that encourages growth and self-esteem.

Finally, seek support when needed. Parenting can be

challenging, and it's okay to ask for help. If you're struggling to manage your child's emotional outbursts or are concerned about their emotional development, don't hesitate to reach out to a pediatrician, child psychologist, or other relevant professionals. These experts can offer valuable guidance and strategies tailored to your child's specific needs. They can also provide you with additional tools and techniques to support your child's journey toward emotional self-

regulation. This isn't a sign of weakness; it's a sign of

strength, acknowledging the importance of seeking support to nurture your child's emotional well-being. The goal is to create a loving and supportive environment where your child feels safe to express their emotions, learn coping strategies, and grow into a emotionally resilient and well-adjusted

individual. This investment in their emotional well-being is a gift that will last a lifetime.

11

Building Resilience and Coping Mechanisms

The transition from preschool to the early elementary years (ages six to eight) marks another significant shift in emotional development. While the foundations of emotional self-regulation laid in the preschool years are crucial, this stage requires a more nuanced approach. Children are now navigating a more complex social landscape, facing increasing academic pressures, and grappling with a wider range of emotions. It's no longer just about managing tantrums; it's about equipping them with the sophisticated tools they need to navigate the intricate world of friendships, school dynamics, and the ever-growing demands of their environment. Think of it as moving from building the scaffolding to installing the intricate plumbing and electrical systems within that skyscraper.

One of the most critical aspects of this developmental stage is building resilience. Resilience isn't simply about bouncing back from adversity; it's about adapting, learning, and growing from challenges. It's about developing a mindset that views setbacks not as insurmountable obstacles, but as opportunities for learning and growth. This involves teaching children to view difficulties as temporary, specific, and external rather than permanent, pervasive, and personal—a cognitive reframing technique known as the "ABC" model. Helping children understand that their failures are not reflections of their inherent worth, but rather specific events that can be learned from, is crucial in fostering resilience.

Practical strategies for building resilience include fostering a growth mindset. This involves emphasizing effort and perseverance over innate ability. Praise should focus on the process and effort invested, rather than solely on the

outcome. For instance, instead of saying "You're so smart!" after a successful project, try "I'm so impressed by how hard you worked on that project! You really persevered." This subtly shifts the focus from inherent ability to effort and dedication, fostering a belief in their capacity for

improvement and growth.

Another key component of building resilience is cultivating problem-solving skills. This involves teaching children a structured approach to tackling challenges. Start by

encouraging them to identify the problem clearly, brainstorm possible solutions, evaluate the pros and cons of each

solution, and finally, implement and evaluate their chosen solution. Role-playing scenarios can be incredibly effective in this process. For example, imagine a scenario where a child's friend takes their favorite toy without asking. You can guide them through the problem-solving process by asking: "What's the problem? How does it make you feel? What are some ways you could handle this situation? What are the possible outcomes of each approach?" This helps them

develop critical thinking and decision-making skills.

Conflict resolution is another essential skill to develop

during these years. Children at this age are increasingly involved in social interactions that can lead to

disagreements. Teaching them effective strategies for

resolving conflicts peacefully is vital for their social and emotional well-being. This involves teaching them to listen actively to the other person's perspective, express their own feelings assertively but respectfully, and collaboratively find solutions that work for everyone involved. Emphasizing empathy is key here; helping them understand and appreciate another person's point of view is fundamental to peaceful conflict resolution. Techniques such as "I" statements ("I feel hurt when...") can be practiced to facilitate clear and non-blaming communication.

Beyond conflict resolution, developing coping mechanisms for stress and setbacks is paramount. Teaching children relaxation techniques like deep breathing exercises, mindfulness activities, or progressive muscle relaxation can be highly beneficial. These techniques help them calm their nervous systems and regulate their emotions when faced with challenging situations. Creating a safe space where children can express their feelings without judgment is also crucial. This could be a designated quiet corner in their room, or simply a time set aside each day for them to talk about their experiences and feelings. Active listening and validation are essential here; simply acknowledging their feelings can be incredibly powerful in helping them feel heard and understood.

Furthermore, expanding their emotional vocabulary is crucial. Children at this age are developing more complex emotional experiences, but their ability to articulate those feelings may still be limited. Teaching them a rich vocabulary to describe their emotions—beyond simply "happy" or "sad"—helps them better understand and manage their internal world. Introduce words like frustrated, anxious, excited, disappointed, bewildered, and proud. Using picture books that depict a range of emotions can be a fun and effective way to broaden their emotional lexicon. Engage in discussions about characters' feelings in stories, encouraging them to identify the emotions and explain why the character might be feeling that way.

Remember, teaching children to cope with stress and bounce back from setbacks is an ongoing process. It requires
consistent modeling and practice. Parents and caregivers should strive to model healthy coping strategies themselves, demonstrating how they handle their own stress and
challenges. This can range from acknowledging difficult
feelings to engaging in relaxation techniques in front of their children. Seeing their parents manage their emotions
effectively provides a powerful learning experience and encourages the children to adopt similar behaviors.

Beyond direct teaching, creating a supportive and nurturing environment is essential. A home filled with unconditional love, acceptance, and understanding forms the bedrock upon which resilience is built. Children who feel safe, secure, and loved are better equipped to navigate life's challenges.

Encourage open communication, creating a space where they feel comfortable expressing their thoughts and feelings
without fear of judgment. This consistent sense of security helps them develop a strong sense of self-worth and fosters their ability to cope with difficult situations.

Incorporating play into emotional development is vital. Play provides a safe and natural context for children to explore various emotions, experiment with coping strategies, and develop social skills. Role-playing, storytelling, and
imaginative games all offer opportunities for children to process their experiences and build emotional resilience.

Encourage participation in group activities that foster cooperation and collaboration, promoting healthy social interactions and emotional regulation.

Lastly, seek professional support when needed. Every child develops at their own pace, and it's essential to recognize when professional guidance may be beneficial. If you observe consistent difficulties in managing emotions, persistent behavioral challenges, or signs of significant distress, consult a child psychologist or other mental health professional. Early intervention can prevent larger issues from developing, ensuring your child's healthy emotional growth. Remember, seeking professional help is a sign of strength and commitment to your child's well-being. It's an

investment in their future emotional health and a testament to your dedication as a parent. This journey of emotional development is a collaborative effort, and you're not alone in navigating its complexities.

12

Navigating Social and Academic Pressures

Late childhood, spanning the ages of nine to twelve, marks a significant transition. The relatively simpler emotional landscape of early childhood gives way to a more complex terrain, shaped by burgeoning social circles, escalating academic demands, and the ever-present pressure to conform. This is a period where children strive for independence, yet simultaneously crave the security and reassurance of their parents' love and guidance. Navigating this delicate balance requires a parental approach that is both supportive and empowering.

The social world expands dramatically during these years. Children are no longer just interacting with a small group of familiar faces; they're navigating larger social networks, grappling with the nuances of friendships, cliques, and social hierarchies. The playground dynamics that once seemed manageable now feel like a complex chess game, replete with shifting alliances, rivalries, and the ever-present threat of exclusion. This can lead to increased anxieties, feelings of inadequacy, and a heightened sensitivity to social cues. A child who previously felt secure might suddenly find themselves struggling to fit in, experiencing feelings of loneliness or even depression.

Parents can play a crucial role in helping their children navigate these choppy social waters. Open and honest
conversations are paramount. Encourage your child to talk about their experiences at school, their friendships, and any challenges they're facing. Active listening, without judgment or interruption, is key. Let them know that their feelings are valid, even if their perceptions of situations might seem skewed. Avoid dismissing their concerns with phrases like

"Oh, don't worry about it" or "Just ignore them." Instead, validate their feelings by saying things like, "That sounds really frustrating," or "I can see why you'd feel hurt by that."

Helping children develop strong social skills is also crucial.

This involves more than just teaching them "please" and "thank you." It's about fostering empathy, teaching them how to resolve conflicts peacefully, and encouraging them to consider other people's perspectives. Role-playing different social scenarios can be immensely helpful. For example, you can practice navigating a situation where a friend has
borrowed something and hasn't returned it, or how to
respond if someone is being unkind. These exercises equip children with the practical skills they need to navigate social complexities effectively.

Academic pressures also intensify during this period. The curriculum becomes more demanding, the workload
increases, and the stakes seem higher. Children are
increasingly evaluated based on their academic performance, and this can trigger stress, anxiety, and even feelings of inadequacy. The pressure to achieve good grades can lead to unhealthy coping mechanisms, such as procrastination,
avoidance, or even cheating. Parents must emphasize the importance of effort and learning over grades. This means celebrating their child's dedication and perseverance, rather than solely focusing on

test scores. Encourage a growth mindset, emphasizing that intelligence is not fixed but can be developed through hard work and effort.

Creating a supportive and structured learning environment at home is equally important. This doesn't necessarily mean sitting down with your child every night and meticulously reviewing their homework. Instead, it involves creating a space where they can focus on their studies without distractions, providing them with the necessary resources and support, and fostering a positive attitude towards learning. Regular communication with their teachers is essential, enabling you to stay informed about their progress, identify any challenges they might be facing, and work collaboratively to find solutions.

The issue of bullying often looms large during this developmental stage. Children may be victims of bullying, or they may even become bullies themselves. In either case, it's crucial to address the situation promptly and effectively. Open communication is vital; create a safe space where your child feels comfortable disclosing any instances of bullying.

If your child is a victim, help them understand that it's not their fault and that they deserve to feel safe and respected.

Encourage them to report bullying incidents to a trusted adult, such as a teacher or counselor. If your child is involved in bullying, it is crucial to address the underlying reasons for their behavior. This might involve exploring any issues with self-esteem, anger management, or social skills deficits. Professional help may be required in such instances.

Building self-esteem is paramount during late childhood. Children are increasingly aware of their self-image and how others perceive them. This is a crucial period to foster a positive sense of self-worth. Encourage their participation in activities they enjoy, whether it's sports, music, art, or anything else that allows them to express themselves and discover

their talents. Celebrate their accomplishments, big and small, emphasizing effort and perseverance over
perfection. Help them identify their strengths and
weaknesses, fostering a realistic self-perception and
encouraging a focus on personal growth.

Remember that this period is also a time of significant
physical changes. The onset of puberty can bring about a host of emotional and physical changes, leading to increased
self-consciousness and emotional volatility. Parents must be patient and understanding, providing a supportive
environment where children feel comfortable exploring their identities and expressing their emotions. Open and honest conversations about puberty and its associated changes are vital, empowering children to navigate these transitions with confidence and self-acceptance.

The importance of providing consistent, unconditional love and acceptance cannot be overstated. Children during this stage need to know that they are loved and valued for who they are, regardless of their academic achievements, social status, or any temporary setbacks they may face. This
unwavering support provides a secure base from which they can explore their identities, navigate challenges, and develop into confident, well-adjusted young adults. The role of the parent is not just to provide solutions, but to help children develop the resilience, problem-solving skills, and self-compassion they need to overcome difficulties and flourish.

Late childhood is a time of incredible growth and
development, brimming with both challenges and
opportunities. By providing a supportive and understanding environment, fostering open communication, and equipping children with the necessary social and emotional skills, parents can help them navigate the complexities of this period, building a strong foundation for their future well-being and success. Remember, you are not alone in

this journey. Seeking professional guidance when needed is a sign of strength, not weakness. It's an investment in your child's happiness and future success. Utilize available

resources, connect with support groups, and embrace the collaborative effort it takes to raise emotionally healthy and resilient children. This journey, although demanding, is also incredibly rewarding, offering countless moments of joy, pride, and the deep satisfaction of witnessing your child's

growth and blossoming into their unique and wonderful selves. Remember to celebrate the small victories along the way and never underestimate the power of your love and unwavering support. It is the foundation upon which their confidence, resilience, and emotional well-being will be built. The challenges may be significant, but the rewards are immeasurable.

13

Supporting Your Child Through Transitions

Change is the only constant in life, and this holds especially true for the ever-evolving landscape of childhood. From the seemingly small shifts, like starting a new school year or moving to a new house, to the more significant upheavals, such as a family relocation or the arrival of a new sibling, transitions are inevitable. How we, as parents, navigate these changes with our children profoundly impacts their
emotional well-being and their ability to develop resilience. The key isn't to prevent change – that's impossible – but to equip our children with the tools and emotional support they need to weather the storms and emerge stronger on the other side.

The initial reaction to change, particularly in younger children, is often fear of the unknown. This fear can manifest in various ways, from clinginess and increased anxiety to regression in previously mastered skills, such as potty
training or sleeping independently. Understanding this
underlying fear is crucial. It's not about being spoiled or difficult; it's about feeling a loss of control and security in a world that suddenly feels uncertain.

Imagine, for instance, the upheaval of moving to a new city.

For a child, their familiar world—their school, friends, play-ground, even the layout of their bedroom—is suddenly uprooted. The familiar comfort they derived from these elements is replaced with uncertainty and a sense of

disorientation. This isn't just about adjusting to a new house; it's about adapting to a completely new social landscape, a different school system, potentially a different language, and a new set of social rules. This is a monumental shift for a

child, and their emotional responses should be understood and validated, not dismissed.

A proactive approach to managing these transitions is vital.

Begin the process well in advance of the actual event. For the aforementioned move, weeks or even months before the relocation, involve your child in the preparation. Show them pictures of the new house, perhaps through virtual tours or even a visit if possible. Talk about the new school, research it together, and find information on-line. Let them choose some aspects of their new room, allowing them to exercise a sense of control in a situation where they feel powerless.

This sense of agency, of being a participant rather than a passive recipient of change, significantly eases anxiety.

During the actual transition, maintain a consistent routine as much as possible. Familiar bedtime stories, preferred meals, and es-tablished family rituals can provide anchors of

stability in an otherwise tumultuous sea of change.

Acknowledge your child's feelings, even if they seem

irrational to you. Phrases like, "I understand you're feeling scared about the move. It's okay to feel that way. Moving is big, and it's per-fectly normal to feel a little nervous," validate their emotions and cre-ate a safe space for them to express their anxieties. Avoid dismissing their feelings with phrases like, "Don't be silly," or, "It's not that bad." These dismissals invalidate their experiences and can damage your connection.

For older children transitioning to middle school or high school, the challenges shift slightly. While the fear of the unknown remains a factor, it's often intertwined with social anxieties – fitting in, navigating complex social dynamics, and managing increased academic pressure. These adolescents are dealing with the development of their identity, and a major change can disrupt this delicate process.

Helping your child navigate these transitions requires a sensitive approach. Encourage them to talk about their concerns, providing a non-judgmental listening ear. Help them develop coping mechanisms. Deep breathing exercises, mindfulness techniques, and even simple journaling can be powerful tools in managing stress and anxiety. Furthermore, connect them with potential support systems. Encourage them to connect with other students, join clubs or teams, or participate in activities that align with their interests. This helps build social connections and reduces feelings of isolation.

Another significant transition often faced by families is the arrival of a new sibling. This can be particularly challenging for older children who have previously enjoyed undivided parental attention. Suddenly, they have to share their parents' love and resources, which can trigger feelings of jealousy, resentment, and even anger. Again, open communication and validation are key. Acknowledge their feelings, letting them know it's perfectly normal to feel a little jealous or upset.

Explain that while the new baby needs a lot of attention, your love for them hasn't diminished. Involve them in the baby's care in age-appropriate ways, giving them a sense of responsibility and ownership. This can help foster a sense of connection rather than competition. Moreover, maintain one-on-one time with the older child, ensuring they don't feel neglected or forgotten.

Remember, the strategies for supporting your child through transitions aren't about fixing the situation, but about supporting *them*

. It's about equipping them with the
emotional resilience to handle change, to adapt to new circumstances, and to grow from these experiences.

Transitions are inevitable, but they also represent opportunities for growth, fostering independence,
adaptability, and emotional strength. By providing a secure, supportive, and understanding environment, we can guide our children through these periods of change, helping them to not just survive, but thrive.

Changes in family dynamics, such as divorce or separation, present even more complex challenges. These transitions often involve a significant loss of stability and routine, and children may experience a wide range of emotions including grief, confusion, anger, and fear. It is crucial to approach these situations with sensitivity, understanding, and open communication. Ensure that your child feels safe and loved, and that they have a consistent support system. Reassure them that despite the changes, they are still loved and
valued. Avoid involving them in adult conflicts and refrain from using disparaging language about the other parent.

Children often internalize conflict and blame themselves.

Consider professional support from a child psychologist or family therapist to help navigate the complex emotions involved in family separations or significant life changes. These professionals provide valuable tools and strategies for coping with difficult situations and building strong family relationships. Their guidance can empower parents to
navigate difficult conversations, set healthy boundaries, and ensure that children's emotional needs are met during these challenging times.

Throughout all these transitions, remember the importance of consistency and predictability. While change is inevitable, a sense of routine and stability provides a crucial anchor for children. Maintaining familiar bedtime routines, family meals, and other cherished traditions can offer a sense of normalcy and comfort, even amidst significant upheaval.

Incorporating calming activities like reading, listening to music, or engaging in creative activities can help reduce

anxiety and provide a sense of peace. Remember, modeling healthy coping mechanisms is crucial. Children often learn by observing their parents, so demonstrating your own ability to manage stress and adapt to change can be

incredibly beneficial.

Finally, celebrate the small victories. Each step forward, no matter how small, is a testament to your child's resilience and growth. Acknowledge their efforts, praise their bravery, and celebrate their achievements. These small acts of

affirmation can build confidence and self-esteem,

empowering them to face future challenges with greater courage and resilience. The journey of raising children is full of transitions, and while challenging, it's also incredibly rewarding. By understanding your child's emotional needs and providing consistent support, you can help them

navigate the ups and downs of life, building a strong

foundation for their future happiness and success.

Remember, you are not alone in this journey. Seek support when needed, embrace the power of community, and celebrate the incredible resilience of your child.

14

Understanding Different Communication Styles

Understanding the intricate dance of communication within a family, particularly bridging the gap between generations, requires a nuanced understanding of diverse communication styles. Children, especially, don't always express themselves in the same way adults do, leading to misunderstandings and frustration on both sides. This often stems from

developmental differences in cognitive abilities, emotional maturity, and social experience. A five-year-old

communicates differently than a teenager, just as a teenager communicates differently than their parents. Recognizing these differences is the first step toward fostering effective and empathetic communication.

Let's consider the preschooler, whose primary mode of communication is often nonverbal. A tantrum, for example, isn't simply a bid for attention; it's frequently a powerful, albeit chaotic, expression of overwhelming emotions—frustration, exhaustion, or even hunger—that the child lacks the vocabulary to articulate. Adults, conditioned to prioritize verbal communication, might initially miss the underlying message, responding with frustration or criticism rather than understanding and empathy. To effectively bridge this gap, parents need to learn to "read" their child's nonverbal cues:

clenched fists, furrowed brows, slumped shoulders, or even a subtle change in tone of voice can all signal underlying emotional states. Active observation, coupled with an
empathetic response ("It looks like you're really frustrated right now. Can you tell me what's wrong?"), can
significantly improve communication.

The teenage years present a unique communication challenge. Teenagers, navigating the turbulent waters of
puberty and identity formation, often communicate indirectly, relying on sarcasm, subtle cues, and even silence to convey their messages. Their desire for autonomy and independence can manifest as resistance to direct
communication, making it challenging for parents to understand their needs and concerns. For example, a teenager's seemingly dismissive response to a parent's inquiry ("Fine.") might mask deeper anxieties or insecurities.

Parents might unintentionally escalate the situation by reacting with irritation or demanding explanations, thereby shutting down communication further. Effective communication in these instances requires patience, active listening, and a willingness to decode the unspoken messages. Open-ended questions ("How was school today?" instead of "Did you get good grades?") can encourage more expansive conversations.

Furthermore, consider the differing communication styles stemming from personality traits. Some children are naturally outgoing and expressive, while others are shy and reserved. An extroverted child might openly express their needs and opinions, while an introverted child might bottle up their emotions, leading to passive-aggressive behavior or emotional withdrawal. Parents need to adapt their communication style accordingly, being sensitive to their child's unique personality. Pushing an introverted child to openly express their feelings might only increase their anxiety, while neglecting to give an extroverted child enough space might lead to frustration and misbehavior.

Understanding personality differences and tailoring communication accordingly is paramount. This might involve employing different techniques for each child—using more visual aids or storytelling for a visual learner, or engaging in quiet, one-on-one conversations for a more reflective child.

Generational differences also play a significant role in shaping communication styles. Parents, raised in a different era with different social norms and technological advancements, might not always understand the nuances of modern communication, including texting, social media, and online interactions. For instance, a parent might misunderstand a teenager's online interactions, interpreting a casual tone as dismissive or disrespectful. Conversely, a teenager might perceive their parent's direct and frank communication as overly critical or controlling. Bridging this generational gap requires mutual understanding, willingness to learn each other's communication preferences, and a conscious effort to avoid making assumptions or judgments.

Effective communication also necessitates a clear understanding of the recipient's emotional state. Before launching into a conversation, especially one involving potentially sensitive topics, consider the child's emotional capacity. If they're upset, stressed, or tired, they're less likely to engage in a constructive conversation. It's crucial to first create a calm and receptive environment before broaching potentially difficult subjects. This might involve taking a break, engaging in a calming activity, or simply waiting until the child is more emotionally regulated. This applies to parents as well. If a parent is feeling overwhelmed or stressed, it's important to acknowledge their emotions and seek support before attempting to engage with their child.

Creating a space where both parent and child feel
comfortable and understood is fundamental for healthy communication.

The language we use also significantly influences
communication effectiveness. Avoid using jargon, complex language, or overly technical terms that a child might not comprehend. Instead, employ simple, direct language that is

tailored to the child's age and understanding. For instance, explaining complex issues like death or divorce requires sensitivity and age-appropriate language. Furthermore, avoid using accusatory or judgmental language that might shut down communication. Replace phrases like "You always..." or "You never..." with more constructive language that
focuses on specific behaviors and their consequences.

Phrases like, "I noticed that..." or "I'm concerned because..."can help initiate a discussion without placing blame or
causing defensiveness.

Beyond the verbal aspects, nonverbal communication holds immense power. Body language, facial expressions, and tone of voice often communicate more than words themselves. A dismissive tone, even when accompanied by reassuring words, can send a completely opposite message. Paying close attention to nonverbal cues – both our own and our child's – is crucial for ensuring that our intended message aligns with the message received. For instance, maintaining eye contact, using an open and relaxed posture, and
matching your tone of voice to your message can convey genuine empathy and understanding. Similarly, recognizing a child's slumped shoulders or averted gaze can signal that something is bothering them, prompting further
investigation.

Finally, effective communication requires active listening—truly hearing what the child is saying, both verbally and nonverbally. This means listening without interrupting, offering unsolicited advice, or judging. Instead, focus on understanding the child's perspective, even if it differs from your own. Reflecting back what the child has said ("So, you're saying you're feeling frustrated because...") can demonstrate your attentiveness and encourage further communication. Active listening fosters trust and respect, creating a safe space where children feel comfortable expressing themselves without fear of judgment or rejection.

It empowers them to feel heard and understood, strengthening the parent-child bond. This active listening is not a passive activity; it requires conscious effort and a commitment to understanding the child's perspective before responding. It might even require setting aside your own immediate reactions and emotions to truly hear the message being conveyed.

In conclusion, understanding the diverse communication styles of children is not merely about mastering techniques but about cultivating empathy, patience, and a genuine desire to connect. It's about acknowledging the developmental stages, personality traits, and generational differences that influence how children express themselves. By learning to navigate these nuances, parents can bridge the communication gap, building strong and lasting relationships based on mutual understanding, trust, and respect. The journey towards effective communication is continuous, requiring ongoing learning, adaptation, and a willingness to grow alongside our children. This investment in understanding will reap immeasurable rewards in the form of stronger family bonds and healthier relationships.

15

The Unspoken Language

The previous chapters explored the diverse ways children communicate, highlighting the vast differences between a five-year-old's expressive capabilities and those of a
teenager, or even the communication styles inherent in different generations. But effective communication isn't solely about the words we use; it's deeply intertwined with the unspoken language—the nonverbal cues that often speak louder than any verbal articulation. This unspoken language forms a significant bridge, or a chasm, depending on our understanding, in the generational gap.

Consider this scenario: you've just finished a long day at work, feeling exhausted and stressed. Your teenager,
absorbed in their phone, barely acknowledges your presence.

You ask about their day, and receive a mumbled,
monosyllabic response. The words themselves might seem insignificant, but the accompanying nonverbal cues paint a far more complex picture. The slumped posture, the averted gaze, the sigh that escapes before the mumbled reply—these all scream something quite different from the simple "Fine." They tell a story of teenage rebellion, frustration, or maybe just overwhelming exhaustion mirroring your own.

Understanding this silent narrative is crucial for effective communication, for connecting on a level far deeper than the surface exchange of words.

Nonverbal communication encompasses a wide spectrum of signals, each subtly influencing the overall message. Body language – the posture, gestures, and even the subtle shifts in weight – forms a significant portion of this unspoken

conversation. A child's slumped shoulders might indicate sadness or defeat, while clenched fists suggest anger or

frustration. A wide, open posture, conversely, often suggests openness, confidence, and a willingness to engage. Observe a child carefully, noting these subtle shifts. A child who suddenly crosses their arms during a conversation may be feeling defensive or unwilling to participate further.

Conversely, mirroring a child's body language can create a sense of rapport and trust, a nonverbal echo of understanding and connection.

Facial expressions are equally powerful communicators. A furrowed brow often translates to confusion or worry; a tight-lipped smile might mask underlying tension or

reluctance. Tears, of course, speak volumes, signifying sadness, hurt, or anger, but their interpretation must be considered within the entire communicative context.

Sometimes, a single tear rolling down a cheek reflects quiet contemplation, rather than overwhelming sorrow.

Recognizing the subtle nuances of facial expressions requires practice and an empathetic approach; rushing to judgment based on a single facial cue can create

misunderstandings and damage trust.

Tone of voice is yet another crucial component of nonverbal communication. The same words spoken in a harsh,

accusatory tone carry a vastly different message compared to those delivered in a calm, reassuring voice. A sharp, raised voice can escalate a conflict instantly, creating defensiveness and shutting down communication. A soft, gentle tone, on the other hand, fosters a sense of safety and encourages open dialogue. Parents often inadvertently create barriers to communication through the tone of their voice, without ever considering the impact of their delivery. Imagine asking a child, "Did you finish your homework?" with an impatient tone. The child, even if they completed their homework, might become defensive and reluctant to share. However, a

calm and caring tone—even when asking a similar question—creates a more inviting and communicative environment.

Beyond these major components, there is a wealth of more subtle nonverbal cues. The distance a child maintains during a conversation – proxemics – can reveal much about their comfort level. A child who consistently stands far away might feel uncomfortable or anxious, while one who stands too close might be seeking excessive reassurance or

attention. Eye contact too, plays a vital role. While

consistent, direct eye contact can signal confidence and engagement, an avoidance of eye contact might signal

shyness, insecurity, or even deception. However, cultural differences regarding eye contact must also be taken into account, as some cultures value direct eye contact less than others.

Interpreting these nonverbal cues accurately requires

mindful observation and a willingness to step into your child's emotional world. Avoid making assumptions based solely on one nonverbal cue; instead, consider the whole picture – the combination of body language, facial

expression, tone of voice, and context. For example, if your child is slumped over with their arms crossed and avoiding eye contact, it's unlikely they're simply tired. A deeper exploration into the underlying emotions might uncover feelings of frustration, sadness, or anger that are preventing open communication. This holistic approach is crucial for accurate interpretation.

Moreover, mastering nonverbal communication isn't just about interpreting your child's cues; it's equally important to be mindful of your own nonverbal communication. Children are acutely sensitive to their parents' body language and tone of voice. A tense posture or impatient tone can instantly shut down a conversation, creating a barrier to open and honest

communication. By being aware of your own nonverbal cues, you can create a safe and welcoming space for your child to express their thoughts and feelings without fear of judgment or reprisal.

Parents can engage in active nonverbal listening – mirroring their child's posture subtly, maintaining appropriate eye contact, and using their own facial expressions to show empathy and understanding. A simple nod of understanding, a concerned frown reflecting their child's worry, or a gentle smile signifying approval can make a world of difference. This creates a sense of connection and validates the child's feelings, fostering a deeper level of trust and rapport.

Practice active listening, consciously matching your body language to your child's. If they're speaking quietly and slowly, mirror their pace and volume. If they're leaning in, lean in as well. This creates a sense of connection and

validates their feelings, conveying a message of empathy and understanding without the need for words. However, avoid mimicking your child's nonverbal cues in an exaggerated manner as this can appear mocking or insincere. The goal is to create a connection, not a caricature.

The development of this intuitive understanding of nonverbal communication often emerges from consistent and empathetic interaction. The more time you spend observing and responding to your child's nonverbal cues, the more adept you will become at deciphering their unspoken

messages. However, this is not a skill learned overnight; it is developed through years of patient observation, empathetic responses, and a conscious effort to connect on a deeper, nonverbal level.

Consider using games and activities to improve nonverbal communication skills. Play charades or Pictionary to encourage children to express themselves nonverbally. You can even introduce a 'silent day' where family members are encouraged to communicate solely through nonverbal cues. This playful approach can make learning about nonverbal communication fun and engaging for both parents and children.

Through observation, conscious reflection and active listening, parents can transform their understanding of nonverbal communication from a mysterious enigma into a powerful tool for connecting with their children. Mastering this unspoken language isn't about deciphering secret codes; it's about learning to read the subtle cues of a child's emotional landscape—a journey of mutual understanding and trust that will enrich your relationship immeasurably. This journey will deepen your understanding of your child, build stronger bonds, and pave the way for more effective and fulfilling communication throughout your child's life, and beyond, strengthening the family unit far beyond what words alone can express.

16

Balancing Love and Discipline

Building healthy boundaries with children is a delicate dance, a careful choreography between unwavering love and firm, consistent discipline. It's a process that evolves with the child's age and understanding, demanding flexibility and a deep understanding of their developmental stage. The goal isn't to create a rigid, authoritarian environment, but rather a nurturing space where children learn self-control, respect for themselves and others, and the crucial life skill of understanding limitations.

Think of boundaries as the sturdy frame of a house. The house itself, filled with warmth, laughter, and unconditional love, represents the parent-child relationship. Without the frame, the house is unstable, prone to collapse under stress.

Similarly, without clear boundaries, the parent-child relationship risks becoming chaotic, leaving children feeling insecure and overwhelmed.

The first crucial step in setting healthy boundaries is establishing clear expectations. This isn't about creating a laundry list of rules; instead, it's about communicating values and guiding principles. For a young child, this might involve setting clear rules about bedtime, mealtimes, and respecting personal space. For a teenager, it could mean discussing responsible social media use, curfews, and academic expectations. The key is to be age-appropriate and to clearly articulate the reasons behind these expectations.

Avoid simply stating rules as dictates; instead, explain the rationale behind them. For instance, instead of saying "No screen time after 8 pm," you might explain, "Getting enough sleep is essential for your health and well-being; that's why we have a screen-time curfew." This approach encourages

understanding and buy-in, fostering cooperation instead of resentment.

Consistency is the cornerstone of effective boundary-setting.

Once expectations are established, it's critical to enforce them consistently. Children thrive on predictability. If a rule is broken, the consequence should be applied fairly and consistently, regardless of the child's mood or your own.

This doesn't mean being inflexible or unyielding. It means being steadfast in your commitment to the established

boundaries, providing a sense of security and stability for your child. Inconsistency breeds confusion and undermines your authority. Children will quickly learn to test boundaries if they perceive inconsistency. A child who is allowed to stay up late one night but punished for it the next will quickly learn to manipulate the situation. Consistency, therefore, is essential for establishing trust and respect.

The consequences for breaking rules should be age-appropriate and proportionate to the infraction. For a young child, a natural consequence might be having to clean up a mess they made. For a teenager, it could involve losing

privileges, such as phone use or social activities. The goal of consequences isn't to punish, but to teach. They should be educational opportunities, designed to help the child

understand the impact of their actions and learn to make better choices in the future. The emphasis should be on

restorative justice, helping repair the situation and fostering a sense of responsibility.

Maintaining a loving relationship while setting boundaries might seem contradictory, but it's essential. Discipline
shouldn't feel punitive or cold; it should stem from a place of love and concern. It's about guiding your child towards maturity and responsibility, teaching them self-discipline and the importance of respecting themselves and others. Even

during disciplinary moments, make time to connect with your child on an emotional level. Acknowledge their
feelings, even if you don't agree with their behavior. This creates a safe space where they feel heard and understood, despite the disciplinary measures. Phrase your corrections with care, focusing on the behavior, not the child. Instead of saying "You're so irresponsible," try "Leaving your toys scattered around creates a hazard. Let's clean them up
together." This subtle shift in language helps foster
understanding and collaboration.

Communication is crucial throughout this process. Explain the rules clearly, and be open to hearing your child's
perspective. This doesn't mean you'll always agree, but it demonstrates respect and creates a dialogue instead of a power struggle. Active listening, discussed in the previous chapter, becomes paramount here. Truly hearing your child's perspective – even if it's an attempt to justify inappropriate behaviour – allows you to address the underlying issues contributing to their actions. Perhaps their outburst stemmed from feeling overwhelmed, ignored, or misunderstood. Understanding the root cause enables you to address not just the behavior but the emotion behind it, strengthening your connection and promoting long-term understanding.

Furthermore, be prepared for your boundaries to evolve as your child grows. What's appropriate for a five-year-old isn't necessarily suitable for a teenager. The principles of clear expectations, consistent consequences, and loving
communication remain, but the specific rules and their

enforcement must be adjusted to reflect your child's
developmental stage and maturity level. This flexibility demonstrates adaptability and keeps your disciplinary
approach relevant and effective.

Consider scenarios where boundaries are tested. Imagine a teenager pushing their curfew. Instead of automatic
punishment, engage in a conversation. Ask why they were late. Actively listen to their explanation, even if you don't agree with their reasoning. If there's a genuine explanation –perhaps a sudden emergency or a missed bus – show
compassion and understanding. However, if it's a recurring issue stemming from poor time management or disregard for the rules, you have the opportunity to address the underlying problem and collaboratively find solutions. This approach emphasizes understanding and problem-solving over simple punitive measures. The conversation becomes a teaching moment, not just a disciplinary one.

Think about younger children testing boundaries with tantrums. While it's tempting to react with frustration or anger, staying calm and remaining consistent is crucial.

Ignore the tantrum (if it's safe to do so), and consistently enforce the consequences for their inappropriate behavior. In this way, you teach them that tantrums won't get them what they want, while simultaneously reinforcing the importance of adhering to established rules. This may take time, but consistency will eventually yield positive results.

Healthy boundaries don't restrict a child's freedom; they provide structure and security. They guide children toward self-regulation, responsibility, and respectful interactions.

They provide a framework within which children can
explore their independence and develop into self-assured, responsible individuals. The goal is not control but
empowerment – enabling children to make sound decisions, navigate challenges, and develop the self-discipline that will serve them well

throughout their lives. The balance between love and discipline is not a compromise but a harmonious blend, where firm guidance fosters growth and unconditional love provides the nurturing environment for flourishing. This

delicate equilibrium is the foundation of a strong, healthy, and lasting parent-child bond. It's a journey that requires patience, understanding, and consistent effort, rewarding parents with a relationship built on mutual respect and

lasting love. It's a testament to the power of effective

communication in creating a nurturing and supportive family environment.

17

Transforming Disagreements into Opportunities

Disagreements are inevitable in any family, but how we navigate these conflicts significantly shapes the parent-child relationship. Transforming disagreements from battles into opportunities for growth and understanding requires a shift in perspective—from seeing conflict as a problem to be solved, to viewing it as a chance to learn, connect, and strengthen the bond. This involves a conscious effort to move beyond simply imposing solutions and instead fostering collaboration and mutual respect.

The foundation of constructive conflict resolution lies in emotional regulation. When tensions rise, our instinctive reactions often escalate the situation. Shouting, criticizing, or resorting to punishment rarely leads to positive outcomes. Instead, consciously taking a deep breath, stepping back for a moment, and acknowledging your own emotions is crucial.

This isn't about suppressing your feelings, but about managing them effectively so you can respond, rather than react. Children are incredibly perceptive, picking up on subtle cues of anxiety or frustration. Modeling calm,

controlled behavior teaches them valuable coping
mechanisms they can utilize in their own lives.

Active listening plays a vital role. Too often, we interrupt, offer unsolicited advice, or jump to conclusions before fully understanding the child's perspective. True listening involves putting aside your own thoughts and feelings, focusing
entirely on the child, and attempting to see the situation through their eyes. This doesn't mean agreeing with their viewpoint, but acknowledging their feelings and validating their experience. Phrases like, "I hear you saying..." or "It sounds like you're feeling..." demonstrate empathy and
show the child that they are being heard and understood.

This act of validation alone can often de-escalate a tense situation. Remember the power of nonverbal communication too – maintain eye contact, nod your head to show you're engaged, and adopt an open and receptive posture.

Once you've truly listened to your child's perspective, it's time to help them articulate their needs and concerns. Often, what begins as a seemingly intractable conflict is rooted in unmet needs – a need for attention, autonomy,
understanding, or simply a sense of belonging. Ask open-ended questions like, "What happened?" "How did that make you feel?" and "What would make things better?" These questions encourage the child to express themselves fully, to identify the underlying issues driving their behavior, and to actively participate in finding a solution. This collaborative approach transforms the child from a passive recipient of rules into an active participant in the decision-making process. This empowers them, fosters a sense of
responsibility, and lays the groundwork for future conflict resolution.

Finding mutually acceptable solutions requires creativity and compromise. It's rarely a case of one person "winning" and the other "losing." The goal is to arrive at a solution that addresses everyone's needs, even if it means making concessions. Brainstorming together can be a helpful approach, encouraging the child to participate in generating potential solutions. Write down all suggestions, even those that initially seem unrealistic. Discuss the pros and cons of each option, helping your child think critically and develop problem-solving skills. The process itself is often as valuable as the final outcome. Even if the initially proposed solution is impractical, the effort of collaborative problem-solving is a powerful lesson in itself.

It's important to remember that setting clear expectations and boundaries doesn't contradict the principle of collaborative conflict resolution. In fact, it reinforces it. When children understand the boundaries within which they operate, they are better equipped to negotiate and resolve disagreements within those parameters. For example, if a child is constantly interrupting conversations, you can collaboratively establish a signal they can use to indicate they wish to contribute without disrupting the flow of conversation. This teaches them self-regulation and respectful communication. It's about finding a balance between allowing children to express themselves and maintaining order and respect.

Following a successful conflict resolution, it is equally important to reflect and reinforce positive behaviors.

Acknowledge the child's efforts to communicate and cooperate. Praise their willingness to find a solution and their ability to compromise. This positive reinforcement encourages them to adopt these constructive conflict resolution skills in future situations. Moreover, reflecting on the process itself is invaluable. Ask questions like, "What did we do well?" or "What could we have done differently?" This metacognitive exercise helps children develop their self-awareness and refine their conflict resolution strategies.

The focus shifts from the specific disagreement to the development of critical life skills.

However, some situations may require parental intervention and guidance. If a child consistently resorts to aggressive or manipulative tactics, it's crucial to intervene firmly but compassionately. Set clear consequences for inappropriate behavior, while still conveying your unwavering love and support. This approach teaches them that their actions have consequences, while also providing a safe space for them to learn and grow. Sometimes, external help might be

necessary. Seeking guidance from a child psychologist or family therapist can offer valuable support and strategies for managing complex conflict situations. They can provide additional tools and techniques for effective communication and conflict resolution, tailoring them to the specific

dynamics of your family. Remember, seeking help is not a sign of weakness, but a testament to your commitment to fostering a healthy and harmonious family environment.

Let's illustrate these principles with an example. Imagine a sibling squabble over a favorite toy. Instead of immediately intervening and assigning blame, take a deep breath and observe the situation. Once the initial outburst subsides, gently approach your children and encourage them to

express their feelings. Ask each child to explain their perspective using "I" statements, for example: "I feel frustrated because Sarah took my toy without asking," rather than "Sarah is always taking my toys!" This helps them to focus on their own emotions and avoid blaming each other. Then, guide them through brainstorming possible solutions. Perhaps they can agree on a set time limit for each child to play with the toy, or they can take turns playing with it. The key is to help them find a solution that works for both of them, promoting compromise and empathy.

Another scenario might involve a teenager arguing against your curfew. Again, active listening is paramount. Hear them out; understand their reasons for wanting a later curfew. Engage in a collaborative conversation. Ask questions like, "What makes you think a later curfew would work for you?" "What are your concerns about the current curfew?"

Together, you could explore options, like a gradual increase in curfew time based on their responsible behaviour, or a more flexible schedule on specific nights. The goal is not to give in, but to work together to find a balance that respects both your concerns and their growing need for autonomy.

This approach fosters a sense of trust and strengthens the parent-child bond.

Remember, conflict is an inherent part of family life; it's the *resolution* that shapes the relationship. By employing these strategies, you're not just resolving a specific disagreement, you're teaching valuable life skills – empathy,

communication, problem-solving, and collaboration. These skills extend far beyond the family dynamic, equipping children to navigate social interactions and challenges

effectively throughout their lives. The journey to effective conflict resolution is a continuous process of learning,

adaptation, and growth—a journey that strengthens the parent-child bond, fosters mutual respect, and creates a supportive, loving environment where disagreements

transform into opportunities for learning and connection. The goal is not the eradication of conflict, but the cultivation of skills to navigate it with grace, understanding, and mutual respect. This approach promotes not only immediate

resolution but also builds resilience and emotional

intelligence in your child, equipping them for the

complexities of life. It's an investment in their future, and in the strength and resilience of your family.

18

Addressing Sensitive Topics with Grace

Difficult conversations are an unavoidable part of parenting. They are the moments that test our patience, challenge our communication skills, and ultimately, define the depth of our connection with our children. These aren't just casual chats; they require careful planning, empathy, and a deep understanding of your child's developmental stage. Whether it's explaining the death of a loved one, navigating the complexities of divorce, or addressing challenging behaviors, the approach you take can profoundly impact their emotional well-being and your relationship.

The first step lies in choosing the right time and place. Avoid launching into a sensitive topic when your child is already stressed, tired, or distracted. Find a quiet, comfortable space where they feel safe and secure. A cozy corner, a favorite reading spot, or even a gentle walk in the park can create a more receptive atmosphere. The environment should communicate calmness and understanding, minimizing distractions that could hinder their ability to process the information. Think of it as creating a sanctuary for this crucial conversation. A rushed conversation, squeezed between errands or shouted across a chaotic kitchen, will likely fall on deaf ears, or worse, create more anxiety.

Next, consider your language. Children, particularly younger ones, understand less of what's said and more of what is felt. Your tone of voice and body language speak volumes, often louder than your words. A gentle, reassuring tone is crucial.

Avoid using overly technical jargon or abstract concepts. Instead, use simple, age-appropriate language that they can easily grasp. Remember to speak honestly, but also with sensitivity. Avoid minimizing their feelings or dismissing

their concerns. Even if you feel the need to downplay the severity of a situation, it's crucial to validate their emotions and show empathy. They might not understand the

complexities of adult issues, but they need to know that their feelings are valid and deserve to be heard.

For example, if you're explaining the death of a pet, avoid clinical descriptions. Instead, focus on the pet's positive qualities, the joy it brought to your family, and the memories you shared. Allow your child to express their grief openly without judgment or pressure to "get over it." Let them know it's okay to cry, to be angry, or to feel confused. This

grieving process can take considerable time, and respecting their emotional journey is paramount.

Similarly, addressing a divorce requires careful consideration. Avoid blaming or criticizing the other parent.

Instead, focus on the practical changes that will occur and reassure your child that they are loved and will continue to receive the same level of care and support. Emphasize the positive aspects of the new arrangement and answer their questions openly and honestly, adapting your explanations to their age and understanding. Children may have different reactions to divorce, ranging from anger to sadness to confusion. Your role is to provide stability, reassuring support, and a constant presence in their lives, regardless of the changes surrounding them.

Dealing with challenging behaviors requires a different approach. Instead of resorting to punishment, focus on understanding the underlying cause of the behavior. Is it a result of stress, frustration, or unmet needs? Engage in active listening, allowing your child to express their feelings without interruption. Once you understand the root cause, you can work together to develop strategies for managing the behavior. This might involve setting clear boundaries, providing positive reinforcement for desired behaviors, and offering alternative ways to express their emotions. This collaborative approach transforms the conversation from a confrontation into a constructive problem-solving session.

Remember, these are not one-time conversations but rather ongoing dialogues. Regular check-ins and open communication channels are essential. Encourage your child to express their thoughts and feelings without fear of judgment or reprisal. Create a safe space where they feel comfortable sharing even the most difficult topics. This continuous dialogue fosters trust and strengthens your bond.

Be prepared for unexpected emotional outbursts or questions. Children process information differently than adults, and their reactions may be unpredictable. Be patient, provide reassurance, and remind them that they are loved and supported.

The key to navigating these difficult conversations lies in your approach. It is not simply about delivering information but about creating a space for empathy, understanding, and mutual respect. Embrace these moments as opportunities to connect with your child, to strengthen your bond, and to equip them with the emotional intelligence needed to navigate the complexities of life. Remember, the goal isn't to avoid these conversations, but to master them, transforming challenging

moments into opportunities for growth,
understanding, and lasting connection.

Consider a scenario where a child is struggling with a peer conflict at school. Instead of dismissing their feelings with "Just ignore them," engage in a conversation. Ask open-ended questions such as, "Tell me more about what
happened. How did that make you feel?" This encourages them to articulate their experiences, helping you understand the root of the problem. Then, guide them through problem-

solving. "What are some ways you could handle this situation differently next time?" This approach empowers them to develop strategies for navigating future conflicts, building resilience and social skills.

Another example might involve a child experiencing anxiety or fear. Instead of simply saying, "Don't be scared," validate their feelings. Acknowledge their fear by saying, "It sounds like you're feeling really anxious. That's okay to feel this way." Then, offer reassurance and help them develop coping mechanisms. This could involve deep breathing exercises, positive self-talk, or even imagining a happy place. This approach not only addresses the immediate concern but equips the child with tools for managing anxiety in the
future. It transforms the conversation from a mere dismissal of their feelings to a collaborative effort in building
resilience and emotional well-being.

In instances where your child is struggling with a specific behavior, such as defiance or aggression, approach the
conversation with a focus on understanding, not punishment.

Instead of immediately reprimanding them, ask, "What happened that made you feel this way?" This encourages introspection and helps you identify the triggers or
underlying emotions contributing to the challenging behavior. Once you understand the cause, you can work together to develop strategies for managing the behavior.

This might involve setting clear expectations, providing positive reinforcement for desired behaviors, and offering alternative ways to express frustration or anger. This
collaborative approach transforms discipline from a punitive measure to a learning experience, strengthening your bond and promoting emotional growth.

The effectiveness of these difficult conversations extends beyond the immediate issue at hand. By demonstrating
empathy, active listening, and collaborative problem-solving, you are modeling crucial life skills for your child. These are the skills they will need to navigate future challenges,
fostering resilience, emotional intelligence, and strong
relationships. This investment in their emotional
development is far-reaching, extending far beyond childhood and into their adult lives, creating a legacy of healthy
communication and effective conflict resolution. The ability to communicate effectively about sensitive topics is a
foundation for building strong, healthy relationships,
fostering trust, and ensuring your child feels seen, heard, and understood—a cornerstone of healthy emotional
development and a loving parent-child bond.

19

Equipping Your Child for Challenges

Life throws curveballs. It's an undeniable truth, especially for our children navigating the complex landscape of
childhood. From playground squabbles to academic hurdles, the challenges they face are formative experiences that shape their character and resilience. Equipping them with the tools to overcome these obstacles, to approach problems not with fear, but with a sense of confident curiosity, is a cornerstone of effective parenting. This isn't about shielding them from hardship – quite the contrary. It's about empowering them to become resourceful, adaptable, and ultimately, triumphant in the face of adversity. This is the essence of teaching problem-solving skills.

The first crucial step in fostering problem-solving abilities is understanding that it's not a singular skill, but a multifaceted process that involves critical thinking, creativity, and
emotional regulation. It's not just about finding
a
solution; it's about learning how to
approach
a problem
systematically, creatively evaluating options, and choosing the best

course of action. Think of it as building a mental toolbox filled with various instruments—each designed to tackle a unique challenge.

One invaluable technique is breaking down large, intimidating problems into smaller, more manageable chunks. Imagine a child struggling with a complex science project. Instead of staring at the mountain of information feeling overwhelmed, we guide them to break it down: first, researching the topic, then outlining the key concepts, then drafting the introduction, then conducting the experiment, and finally, writing the conclusion. Each step is a small victory, contributing to the overall success, making the daunting task less intimidating and more achievable.

This process of decomposition allows children to experience a sense of accomplishment at each stage, building their confidence and reinforcing the idea that complex challenges are solvable through focused effort. This positive reinforcement is crucial; it's the fuel that propels them forward, motivating them to persevere even when faced with setbacks. It's about celebrating the journey, not just the destination. When a child successfully completes a smaller segment of the project, take the time to acknowledge their progress. Say something like, "Wow, look at how much you've already accomplished! You've done a fantastic job researching this topic; your notes are really thorough." This positive feedback encourages them to continue and instills a belief in their ability to tackle the remaining tasks.

Brainstorming is another vital component of effective problem-solving. This is where creativity takes center stage. It's an opportunity for children to unleash their imaginations, to explore multiple perspectives, and to generate a wide array of potential solutions. It's important to create a judgment-free environment during brainstorming. Every idea, no matter how unconventional, should be welcomed and explored. This encourages risk-taking and fosters a willingness to think outside the

box. The goal isn't
necessarily to identify the perfect solution immediately, but to generate a range of possibilities, expanding their thinking and problem-solving horizons.

Once a range of solutions has been brainstormed, the next step involves evaluating the pros and cons of each. This is where critical thinking skills come into play. This process can be fun and engaging by using visual aids, like creating a simple chart to compare and contrast options. Having a child

draw pictures to represent the plus and minus points of each solution can help them visualize and process the information more effectively. Encourage them to ask questions like, "What are the benefits of this solution?", "What are the potential drawbacks?", and "What are the potential

consequences?". These questions not only help in critically evaluating the options but also improve their analytical skills.

Teaching children to anticipate potential consequences is an essential aspect of problem-solving. It's about fostering foresight, helping them understand that their actions have repercussions. Asking "What might happen if..." encourages them to think beyond the immediate outcome and consider the potential long-term effects. This isn't about instilling fear, but rather about equipping them with the ability to make informed choices. For example, if a child is considering not doing their homework, a discussion about the potential consequences—a lower grade, a missed learning opportunity—is vital in guiding them to make the right decision.

Role-playing scenarios can be incredibly effective in
practicing problem-solving skills. This provides a safe space to explore different solutions without the pressure of real-life consequences. You could create a scenario where a child has accidentally broken a friend's toy. Through role-playing, they can explore various ways to address the situation—
apologizing, offering to replace the toy, explaining the

circumstances—and learn to evaluate the effectiveness of each approach. This interactive approach makes learning engaging and helps them develop emotional intelligence, navigating challenging social dynamics effectively.

Another crucial element is encouraging self-reflection. After a problem is solved (or even if a solution wasn't found), it's important for children to reflect on the process. Ask them

questions like: "What did you learn from this experience?","What worked well?", "What could you have done

differently?", and "What strategies could you use next time?". This reflective process helps them internalize their learning, identifying effective techniques and areas needing improvement. It transforms setbacks into valuable learning opportunities, fostering a growth mindset.

Finally, remember that patience is key. Building problem-solving skills is a gradual process, not a race. Children will not always find the optimal solution immediately.

Sometimes they will make mistakes, and that is perfectly acceptable. The aim is to foster a process of learning and improvement, emphasizing that setbacks are opportunities for growth and development. Celebrate their efforts,

encourage persistence, and provide guidance along the way. By creating a supportive and encouraging environment, you are building confidence and instilling a belief in their ability to overcome challenges.

Through consistent practice and encouragement, children can build a strong foundation of problem-solving skills. This empowers them not only to overcome immediate obstacles but also to navigate the complexities of life with confidence and resilience, ultimately shaping them into resourceful and adaptable individuals prepared for whatever the future may hold. This is a gift that will serve them far beyond their childhood years. It's a gift of self-reliance, independence, and the unwavering belief in their own capabilities—a truly priceless inheritance.

20

───────────────

Nurturing a Positive
SelfImage

The foundation of resilience isn't just about problem-solving; it's deeply intertwined with a child's self-esteem. A child who believes in themselves, who knows their worth
regardless of external validation, is far better equipped to navigate the inevitable bumps in the road. This unshakeable belief in their own capabilities is the bedrock upon which resilience is built. It's the quiet confidence that whispers, "I can handle this," even when faced with daunting challenges. Cultivating this self-esteem, this positive self-image, is not a passive process; it requires conscious and consistent effort from parents. It's about creating an environment where a child feels unconditionally loved, accepted, and valued, flaws and all.

Unconditional love is the cornerstone. It means loving your child not for their achievements or their behavior, but simply for who they are – a unique and irreplaceable individual. This isn't about condoning bad behavior; setting boundaries and teaching responsibility are crucial. However, the love remains constant, a steadfast anchor in the stormy seas of childhood. It's the message that reverberates throughout their lives: "I love you, not because you're perfect, but because you are you." This understanding becomes their internal compass, guiding them through moments of self-doubt and uncertainty.

Celebrating achievements, no matter how small, is another vital aspect. A child who masters tying their shoelaces, finishes a challenging puzzle, or performs well in a school play deserves genuine and enthusiastic praise. These moments aren't just about the accomplishment itself; they are opportunities to reinforce their self-worth. The focus should be on their effort, their persistence, and their growth. Instead of simply saying, "Good job!", try phrases like, "I noticed how hard you worked on that puzzle; your perseverance paid off!" or "I'm so proud of the effort you put into your presentation; you clearly put a lot of thought into it." This kind of specific praise highlights not just the outcome, but the process, fostering a sense of accomplishment and self-efficacy.

Equally important is helping children learn from their mistakes. Childhood is a time of exploration and experimentation, often involving inevitable missteps and failures. These are not to be viewed as failures, but as valuable learning experiences. Instead of focusing on the mistake itself, guide your child through a process of self-reflection. Ask questions like, "What happened?", "How did you feel?", and "What could you do differently next time?". This approach helps them understand their mistakes without feeling judged or shamed. It empowers them to take ownership of their actions and to develop strategies for future success. It teaches them that setbacks are temporary and that growth comes from learning from those experiences. It shifts the focus from avoiding mistakes to embracing them as opportunities for growth and learning.

Positive self-talk and affirmations are powerful tools in building a child's self-esteem. Children, just like adults, are susceptible to negative self-talk, often internalizing critical comments or comparing themselves to others. Parents can counteract this by actively promoting positive self-talk. Help your child identify their strengths and talents, reminding them of their positive qualities. You can even create positive affirmations together, writing them down and repeating them regularly. These affirmations can be as simple as "I am kind," "I am strong," or "I am smart." This consistent

reinforcement of positive self-perception can help build confidence and resilience.

Remember that building self-esteem isn't a quick fix; it's an ongoing process that requires consistent effort and patience.

It's about creating a nurturing environment where children feel safe to express themselves, to take risks, and to learn from their mistakes without fear of judgment. The goal is not to shield children from challenges, but to equip them with the internal resources to face those challenges with

confidence and self-belief.

Consider the example of eight-year-old Lily. Lily loves to paint, but recently, she's become hesitant to share her

artwork. She's started comparing her paintings to those of her more advanced art classmate, Maya. Lily's self-esteem is taking a hit because she feels her work doesn't measure up. Instead of dismissing her concerns, her parents engage her in a conversation. They actively listen to her feelings of

inadequacy, validating her emotions without minimizing her concerns. They then help Lily focus on her strengths,

reminding her of the unique style and creativity in her

paintings. They encourage her to explore different

techniques and express her individuality, rather than directly comparing herself to others. They introduce positive

affirmations like, "Lily, your paintings are full of

imagination and colour," and "You are a talented artist, and your style is unique and beautiful." They actively promote her self-belief by displaying her artwork around the house and encouraging her to share it with friends and family, emphasizing the joy of creating, rather than solely the perfection of the product. Through this consistent support and encouragement, Lily's confidence gradually grows. She starts experimenting with different painting styles,

discovering new techniques, and ultimately reclaiming her artistic passion.

Another example: Ten-year-old Tom struggles with math. He gets easily frustrated and tends to give up when faced with challenging problems. His parents, instead of criticizing his performance, focus on his effort and perseverance. They use positive reinforcement, celebrating small victories, like finally understanding a particular concept or solving a

problem independently. They encourage him to break down complex problems into smaller, manageable steps. They emphasize the importance of learning from mistakes, using his errors as an opportunity to improve his problem-solving skills. They praise his persistence and effort even when he doesn't get the right answer immediately. They might say, "I see you're really focusing on this problem; that's fantastic! Let's try a different approach." or "I'm so impressed by your perseverance; you kept trying even when it was challenging. That's what matters most." They actively avoid comparisons with his peers, fostering a growth mindset. They remind him that mistakes are normal and that progress takes time.

Gradually, Tom's confidence in his math abilities improves.

He begins to approach challenges with a more positive attitude, believing in his ability to overcome obstacles. He learns that effort and persistence are just as important, if not more, than achieving immediate success.

These examples illustrate the importance of creating a

nurturing and supportive environment where children are encouraged to express themselves, embrace challenges, and learn from their mistakes. It's not about creating a shield against adversity, but about providing children with the tools and confidence to face adversity head-on, knowing their worth is inherent and unwavering. This is the essence of fostering resilience: building a strong sense of self-esteem that allows children to thrive, not just survive, in the face of life's challenges. It's an investment in their future, a gift that will serve them well long after they leave the nest,

empowering them to navigate the world with confidence, compassion, and an unwavering belief in their own

capabilities. It's about planting a seed of self-belief that will blossom into a lifelong sense of self-worth and resilience. And that, ultimately, is the most valuable gift any parent can give.

21

Managing Emotions and Behavior

The unwavering self-esteem we discussed – that quiet confidence whispering "I can handle this" – is not simply a magical shield against hardship. It's a dynamic force, fueled by the ability to understand and manage one's own emotions and behaviors. Resilience isn't about avoiding emotional storms; it's about navigating them skillfully, with the tools and understanding to weather any tempest. This is where self-regulation comes into play – the ability to control
impulses, manage stress, and respond to challenges in
healthy ways. It's the inner compass guiding a child through emotional turbulence, helping them steer clear of impulsive reactions and make thoughtful choices, even under pressure.

Think of it like learning to ride a bicycle. At first, it's
wobbly, uncertain, and filled with the risk of falls. But with practice, with the guidance of a supportive adult, the child learns to balance, to steer, to navigate the terrain. Self-regulation is much the same. It's a skill that develops over time, honed through practice and patience. It's not about perfection; it's about progress.

One of the most effective tools for cultivating self-regulation is teaching children deep breathing techniques. When a child feels overwhelmed – whether by anger, frustration, or

90

sadness – their body often reacts physically: heart racing, breath quickening, muscles tensing. Deep breathing acts as a counterbalance, a way to calm the physiological storm
brewing within.

Start with simple exercises. Have your child sit comfortably, close their eyes, and focus on their breath. Guide them to inhale slowly and deeply through their nose, filling their

belly with air. Then, have them exhale slowly through their mouth, feeling the tension release with each breath. You can make it fun by counting the breaths together, or by using visual aids, like watching a candle flame flicker as they breathe. Even a five-minute session can make a significant difference. It's a simple yet powerful tool they can use

anytime, anywhere, to regain control.

Mindfulness practices, similar to deep breathing, help
children connect with the present moment, reducing the power of overwhelming emotions. Instead of being swept away by a torrent of feelings, mindfulness allows them to observe their emotions without judgment, like watching clouds drift across the sky. Simple mindfulness exercises, like focusing on the sensations of their feet on the floor or listening to the sounds around them, can help ground them in the present, reducing anxiety and promoting a sense of calm. You can incorporate mindfulness into everyday routines, like during mealtimes or bedtime stories, by encouraging them to pay attention to the sights, sounds, smells, and tastes around them.

Positive self-talk is another crucial component of self-regulation. It's about replacing negative, self-defeating thoughts with positive, encouraging ones. When a child makes a mistake, instead of berating themselves, encourage them to reframe the situation. "I didn't get it right this time, but I can try again," or "It's okay to make mistakes; I'll learn from this." This teaches them resilience in the face of
setbacks, fostering a growth mindset rather than a fixed one.

This isn't about blindly praising everything; it's about validating their feelings while gently guiding them towards a more positive outlook. You can help by modeling positive self-talk yourself. Let them hear you acknowledge your own mistakes and talk yourself through challenges with kindness

and encouragement. Children learn by observing, and modeling this behavior is far more effective than simply telling them to think positively.

Coping strategies are essential tools in a child's self-regulation toolkit. These are specific techniques they can use to manage difficult emotions or situations. For example, if your child gets angry easily, you might teach them to take a "time-out" in a quiet space to calm down, or to engage in a calming activity like drawing or listening to music. If they struggle with anxiety, you might teach them relaxation

techniques like progressive muscle relaxation, where they tense and release different muscle groups.

Remember, the key is to tailor the coping strategies to your child's individual needs and preferences. Some children might find comfort in physical activity, while others prefer creative outlets. The important thing is to empower them with a range of options to choose from depending on the situation.

Developing a consistent routine can also significantly contribute to self-regulation. Predictability provides a sense of security and reduces anxiety. A regular bedtime routine, consistent mealtimes, and established daily schedules can help children feel more in control and less overwhelmed.

This predictability allows them to anticipate events and reduce the potential for emotional outbursts stemming from uncertainty. The sense of order helps them develop a sense of their own rhythm and predictability, enabling them to anticipate needs and plan accordingly.

Furthermore, fostering empathy and emotional literacy plays a crucial role in self-regulation. Helping children understand and label their own emotions, as well as the emotions of others, equips them with the vocabulary and awareness to

manage their feelings effectively. Encourage them to identify what they're feeling and why, and to express their emotions in a healthy way. This process of naming emotions – "I feel frustrated because..." or "I feel sad because..." – allows them to detach from the emotion somewhat, reducing its overwhelming power.

Moreover, teaching conflict resolution skills is essential for self-regulation. Equipping children with the tools to navigate disagreements peacefully and constructively reduces

impulsive reactions and fosters better emotional control.

Role-playing scenarios, practicing active listening, and

learning to compromise are vital skills that promote self-regulation in social situations. These skills extend far beyond childhood, impacting their adult relationships and ability to navigate complex social situations.

Finally, remember that self-regulation is a journey, not a destination. It's a skill that develops gradually over time, with setbacks and successes along the way. Be patient and supportive, celebrating small victories and offering

encouragement during challenging moments. Providing a safe and validating environment where children feel

comfortable expressing their emotions, even the difficult ones, is crucial for fostering self-regulation and building resilience. Your consistent support and understanding will serve as a beacon, guiding them through emotional storms and empowering them to navigate life's challenges with confidence and competence. This process of nurturing self-regulation is an investment in their future happiness, success, and overall well-being, a gift far more valuable than any material possession. It's about empowering them to become the masters of their own emotions, not slaves to them,

ultimately leading to a life lived with greater contentment and resilience.

22

Helping Your Child Cope with Pressure

The ability to navigate the choppy waters of stress is a cornerstone of resilience. It's not about eliminating stress entirely – life, even a child's life, is inherently full of
challenges – but rather equipping your child with the tools to handle those challenges effectively. Think of it like teaching them to surf; you wouldn't keep them from the ocean, but you would certainly teach them how to ride the waves,
avoiding wipeouts and finding the joy in the ride.

One of the most powerful tools in a child's stress-management arsenal is physical activity. The connection between physical exertion and emotional well-being is undeniable. Running, jumping, dancing, swimming – any activity that gets the heart pumping and the blood flowing –acts as a natural stress reliever. Exercise isn't just about burning calories; it's about releasing endorphins, those amazing natural mood boosters that can help alleviate
anxiety and improve overall mood. Think of it as a built-in emotional reset button.

For younger children, think less structured play. A romp in the park, a game of tag, or simply letting loose with some boisterous play is incredibly beneficial. For older children, consider incorporating sports, dance classes, martial arts, or even just a daily walk or bike

ride. The key is to find
something they genuinely enjoy, something that feels more like fun than a chore. It's about building a positive
association with physical activity, so that it becomes a go-to strategy for stress relief, not just another task on their to-do list. Observe your child's preferences and let them guide the selection.

Beyond physical activity, relaxation techniques offer a
powerful pathway to stress reduction. These techniques don't require hours of dedicated practice; even a few minutes a day can make a significant difference. Deep breathing
exercises, for instance, are remarkably effective. Teach your child to breathe deeply from their belly, inhaling slowly and deeply, holding for a few seconds, and then exhaling slowly.

You can make it fun by turning it into a game, maybe
visualizing blowing bubbles or inflating a balloon with each breath.

Guided imagery is another potent tool. Encourage your child to create vivid mental images of peaceful scenes, perhaps a favorite place in nature or a comforting memory. This can be particularly helpful before bed, helping to calm their mind and prepare them for sleep. There are many guided
meditations available online or through apps specifically designed for children, offering calming voices and engaging stories to guide them through the process. The goal isn't to erase all thoughts; it's about gently steering the mind towards calm and serenity.

Progressive muscle relaxation is another technique that can be particularly helpful for older children. This involves tensing and releasing different muscle groups, starting with the toes and working up to the head. The process of
consciously tensing and releasing helps to identify and alleviate muscle tension, which often accompanies stress. Explain the process clearly and make it a shared experience, modeling the technique yourself. This normalizes the
practice and encourages your child to embrace it as a self-care ritual.

The restorative power of nature is often underestimated.

Spending time outdoors can have a profound impact on a child's emotional well-being. The sights, sounds, and smells

of nature have a naturally calming effect, helping to reduce stress and anxiety. A walk in the woods, a picnic in the park, or simply sitting under a tree and observing nature can be incredibly therapeutic. Encourage your child to connect with nature regularly; let them get their hands dirty, climb trees, explore, and discover the wonders of the natural world. This connection to nature becomes a source of solace and

resilience, a place they can retreat to when feeling overwhelmed.

Identifying stressors is a crucial step in developing effective coping mechanisms. Help your child identify the specific situations or events that trigger stress. Is it a difficult test at school? A conflict with a friend? A fear of the dark? Once you've identified these stressors, you can work together to develop personalized coping strategies. These strategies should be age-appropriate and tailored to the specific challenge.

For younger children, visual aids can be incredibly helpful.

A simple chart depicting common stressors and corresponding coping mechanisms can empower them to take charge of their emotional well-being. The chart might include images of calming activities like drawing, reading, or playing with a favorite toy. For older children, problem-solving techniques can be introduced. Encourage them to break down a challenging task into smaller, more manageable steps. This sense of control reduces the overall feeling of overwhelm.

Role-playing can also be a fantastic tool for helping children manage stress. Practice different scenarios with them,

allowing them to role-play different coping strategies. This provides a safe space for them to experiment with different techniques and gain confidence in their ability to handle stressful situations. Remember, these are not just abstract exercises; these are tools to navigate real-life challenges.

Remember the importance of positive self-talk. Help your child identify and challenge negative thoughts. Instead of saying, "I'm going to fail this test," encourage them to reframe it into, "I'm going to do my best, and I've prepared well." Positive self-talk is a powerful tool for building confidence and resilience. It's about changing the internal narrative, moving from a place of fear and doubt to a place of hope and self-belief.

Teaching children stress management techniques isn't a one-time event; it's an ongoing process. Regularly revisit these strategies, adjusting them as needed to meet their evolving needs and challenges. Make it a collaborative effort,
involving them in the decision-making process. Their
ownership of these strategies is key to their effectiveness.

Creating a supportive and understanding environment at home is paramount. Let your child know that it's okay to feel stressed, that these feelings are normal, and that you're there to help them navigate them. Avoid dismissing their feelings or minimizing their concerns. Instead, validate their
emotions, listen actively, and offer your unwavering support.

This creates a safe haven where they feel comfortable expressing themselves without fear of judgment.

Building resilience isn't simply about equipping children with coping mechanisms; it's about fostering a sense of self-efficacy, the belief in their own ability to handle challenges. This belief is cultivated through consistent encouragement, positive feedback, and opportunities for them to succeed. Celebrate their successes, both big and small, highlighting their perseverance and resilience. Focus on their effort and progress, rather than just the outcome.

Remember, setbacks are inevitable. Children will face disappointments and failures along the way. These
experiences, while painful, are valuable learning

opportunities. Help your child view these setbacks as chances to learn and grow, reinforcing the message that resilience involves bouncing back from adversity, not avoiding it altogether. This perspective shift is crucial in building long-term resilience.

Stress management is a crucial life skill, and it's never too early to begin nurturing this ability in your child. By
introducing these techniques early and consistently, you equip them not just for childhood challenges but for a
lifetime of navigating life's ups and downs with grace, strength, and a resilient spirit. The journey might have its bumps, but with your guidance and support, your child will learn to ride those waves with confidence and courage. And that, ultimately, is the greatest gift you can give.

23

Fostering Connections with Others

Building a strong support network for your child is like creating a sturdy safety net – it's there to catch them when they stumble, offering comfort and encouragement during challenging times. This network isn't just about having people around; it's about fostering genuine connections based on trust, empathy, and mutual respect. It's about building a village that surrounds your child with love and understanding, helping them navigate the complexities of life with confidence and resilience.

Family forms the cornerstone of this support system. It's within the family unit that children first learn about love, belonging, and security. Open and honest communication is key. Create a space where your child feels comfortable sharing their thoughts and feelings, knowing they won't be judged or dismissed. Regular family dinners, shared
activities, and even simply cuddling up for a bedtime story can foster a sense of connection and belonging. Encourage siblings to support each other, fostering a bond of
camaraderie and mutual understanding. Remember, family isn't always blood relatives; it's about the people who love and care for your child unconditionally. Foster these
relationships with intentionality.

99

Beyond the immediate family, friends play a vital role in a child's support system. Friends offer a different kind of connection – one built on shared interests, laughter, and mutual respect. They provide opportunities for social interaction, learning how to navigate friendships, resolve conflicts, and build healthy relationships. Encourage your child to develop friendships by creating opportunities for social interaction through playdates, extracurricular

activities, or joining community groups. Help them build healthy friendships by teaching them the importance of empathy, kindness, and respect for others. Teach them to identify and avoid toxic relationships. This doesn't mean shielding them from disagreements, but rather teaching them how to navigate conflict constructively and resolve

differences peacefully.

The community plays a broader, yet equally significant role.

Community involvement provides opportunities for connection, shared experiences, and a sense of belonging.

Encourage your child to participate in community events, volunteer activities, or join clubs and organizations. This exposure expands their social circle, introduces them to different perspectives, and fosters a sense of civic

responsibility. Connecting with other parents within your community can also be invaluable. Sharing experiences, exchanging advice, and offering mutual support can make a significant difference in managing the challenges of

parenthood. This shared experience creates a powerful sense of belonging and can alleviate feelings of isolation.

But building a strong support system isn't a passive endeavor. It requires active participation and nurturing.

Regularly check in with your child, asking about their friendships, their experiences at school, and any challenges they might be facing. Listen actively, showing empathy and understanding. Encourage them to share their feelings,

validating their emotions, even if you don't necessarily agree with them. This creates a safe space where they feel
comfortable seeking support when needed.

Remember that different children thrive in different
environments and require different types of support. Some children are extroverted and flourish in large groups, while others are introverted and prefer smaller, more intimate

settings. Respect your child's personality and preferences, fostering connections that align with their individual needs. A supportive environment isn't about forcing connections but rather creating opportunities for your child to connect authentically.

Navigating conflicts within the support system is inevitable.

Disagreements between friends, family conflicts, or
misunderstandings within the community are all part of life. These situations offer invaluable learning opportunities for your child. Guide them through these challenges, teaching them conflict resolution skills, such as active listening, empathy, and compromise. Show them how to express their feelings respectfully, while also considering the perspectives of others. Help them understand that resolving conflicts is a process, requiring patience and understanding.

Building a strong support system is an ongoing process that evolves as your child grows and their needs change.

Regularly assess the strength of your child's support
network, identifying any gaps or areas needing
improvement. Be flexible and adaptable, adjusting your approach as needed. This isn't a one-size-fits-all solution; it requires ongoing attention and nurturing.

Moreover, be mindful of your own support system as a
parent. You cannot pour from an empty cup. Take care of your own well-being, seeking support when needed. This modeling of self-care provides a powerful example for your child, demonstrating the importance of seeking help and prioritizing mental health. Joining parent support groups, connecting with friends or family members, or

seeking
professional guidance are all valuable ways to replenish your own reserves.

One practical strategy is to actively cultivate connections with other families. Organize playdates, join parent-teacher associations, or participate in school events. This creates opportunities for your child to interact with other children and for you to connect with other parents. These connections can offer invaluable support during challenging times and provide a sense of community.

Another approach is to identify mentors or role models within your child's life. These individuals can provide guidance, inspiration, and a positive influence. These could be teachers, coaches, family friends, or community leaders who embody qualities you admire and want your child to emulate. This broadened perspective exposes them to diverse viewpoints and strengthens their understanding of the world.

For children who struggle with social interactions, consider enrolling them in activities that promote social skills development. This could be anything from team sports to drama classes or art workshops. These environments offer structured opportunities to practice social skills, build self-confidence, and make connections with peers who share similar interests.

Remember, the goal is to create a web of support, a network of individuals who care about your child and are willing to offer help and guidance when needed. This isn't just about solving problems; it's about building a sense of belonging, fostering a feeling of security, and empowering your child to navigate the challenges of life with confidence and
resilience. It's about creating a safety net that allows them to take risks, to learn from their mistakes, and to grow into well-adjusted, capable individuals.

Consider the long-term implications. The support system you help your child build will serve them throughout their life. The ability to form and maintain healthy relationships is crucial for emotional well-being and success in all aspects of life. By fostering strong connections now, you're laying the foundation for a lifetime of support and resilience. And that, ultimately, is the most valuable gift you can give your child. It's a gift that will continue giving long after they've left the nest. This investment in their social and emotional

development will have a lasting impact on their happiness and well-being, shaping them into confident and resilient adults. The journey of building this network will be a

rewarding one, filled with shared laughter, mutual support, and the deep satisfaction of knowing you've provided your child with the strongest possible foundation for a fulfilling life.

24

Effective Strategies for Managing Outbursts

The rollercoaster of parenthood often throws us unexpected loops, and few are as jarring as a full-blown toddler tantrum or a preteen meltdown. These explosive emotional outbursts can leave parents feeling bewildered, frustrated, and even inadequate. But before you reach for the emergency

chocolate stash (we've all been there!), understand that tantrums and meltdowns are normal developmental stages, a crucial part of a child's emotional growth. They are not necessarily signs of a "bad" child, but rather an indication of a child struggling to manage their big feelings. The key lies not in stopping them altogether, which is often impossible, but in learning to navigate them effectively.

Imagine this: Little Lily, a vibrant three-year-old, is building a magnificent tower of blocks. Hours of meticulous work, a testament to her focused concentration. Then, with a

catastrophic thud, the tower collapses. Lily's face crumples. Tears stream down her cheeks. A wail erupts, a symphony of frustration and despair. This isn't willful misbehavior; it's a raw, unfiltered expression of intense emotion. Lily lacks the sophisticated emotional regulation skills to manage her disappointment constructively. This is where parents step in, not as judges, but as guides.

Our first instinct might be to scold her: "Don't be silly, it's just blocks!" But this response dismisses her feelings,
invalidating her experience and potentially exacerbating the situation. Instead, try this: kneel down to her level, make eye contact, and acknowledge her distress. "Oh, Lily, your tower fell. That looks really upsetting. You worked so hard on it, and I can see how disappointed you are." This simple act of validation, of seeing and hearing her feelings, can be

incredibly powerful. It shows empathy, a cornerstone of effective parenting.

The approach to managing tantrums and meltdowns differs based on the child's age. With toddlers, physical comfort often works wonders. A gentle hug, a quiet space to calm down, or even just a reassuring presence can make a
significant difference. For older children, a different strategy is needed. They might require a more verbal approach,
allowing them to express their frustrations and anxieties. Active listening remains paramount – let them talk, even if it seems irrational or repetitive.

Remember, the goal isn't to suppress the emotions but to help the child learn to manage them. This is a skill learned gradually, with patience and consistent support. Provide a safe space for emotional expression. This doesn't necessarily mean letting the tantrum run its course unchecked. It means creating an environment where your child feels understood, not judged. A quiet corner, a comfortable blanket, even a special "calm-down" toy can be invaluable tools.

Once the immediate storm has subsided, engage in a calm discussion about what happened. Help your child identify their feelings ("You were feeling angry and frustrated
because your blocks fell down, right?"). Teach them
alternative ways to express these feelings. For instance, you could introduce simple coping mechanisms like taking deep breaths, squeezing a stress ball, or engaging in a calming activity like drawing. For

older children, encouraging them to verbalize their frustration can help them gain control of the situation before it escalates.

The effectiveness of these strategies hinges on consistency. Establishing clear expectations and boundaries is essential.

Children need to understand that while their feelings are valid, certain behaviors are unacceptable. Consistent discipline, delivered calmly and firmly, reinforces these boundaries. Remember, punishment isn't about making the child feel bad; it's about teaching them how to behave appropriately.

Let's explore some specific examples. Suppose your eight-year-old, Tom, throws a tantrum because he didn't get the video game he wanted. Instead of yelling back, try this: "Tom, I understand you're disappointed you didn't get the game. It's okay to feel sad or angry, but throwing things is not acceptable. Let's talk about why we didn't get it today, and then we can think about other things you could do to feel better." This approach validates his feelings without condoning his behavior.

Or, consider a situation with a younger child. Two-year-old Mia is having a meltdown because she wants another cookie, even though you've already said no. Instead of a power struggle, try distraction: "Mia, it's time for a story! Look at this amazing book!" Or offer a compromise: "You can have one more cookie after dinner." Positive reinforcement, even small gestures of affection after a meltdown subsides, can go a long way in building a positive relationship.

Now, let's dive deeper into the developmental aspects.

Toddler tantrums are often rooted in frustration, exhaustion, or a lack of communication skills. They are essentially a child's way of saying, "I'm overwhelmed, and I don't know how to cope." With toddlers, consistent routines, predictable schedules, and clear expectations can help minimize the frequency of tantrums.

As children enter preschool, their emotional repertoire expands. They begin to understand cause-and-effect relationships, leading to more complex emotional responses.

Teaching them emotional vocabulary ("I'm feeling angry," "I'm feeling sad") empowers them to name and understand their emotions, which is the first step toward managing them. Role-playing scenarios, even with stuffed animals, can help children practice appropriate emotional expressions.

In the elementary school years, social dynamics and academic pressures become significant stressors. Children might experience peer pressure, anxiety about school performance, or emotional reactions to family conflicts. Active listening, clear communication, and building a strong support system become even more crucial. Encourage your child to express their feelings openly, providing a safe space for them to share their anxieties and concerns.

During the preteen and teen years, meltdowns can take on a different form. Hormonal changes, social complexities, and the search for independence can all contribute to emotional outbursts. Parents need to approach these situations with empathy and understanding, acknowledging the developmental shifts and the challenges of adolescence. Open communication and setting healthy boundaries remain vital, but the approach needs to be more collaborative and less directive.

Remember, managing tantrums and meltdowns is not a race to eliminate outbursts entirely. It's a marathon of learning and growing together. Celebrate small victories, acknowledge progress, and remember that you are not alone.

Parenting is challenging, and seeking support from other parents, therapists, or professionals is perfectly acceptable.

Embrace the imperfections, learn from the setbacks, and cherish the moments of connection that emerge amidst the chaos. Because in the heart of those emotional storms, lies the opportunity to forge a deeper understanding, and a stronger bond, with your child.

25

Fostering Cooperation and Understanding

Sibling rivalry. The very words conjure images of squabbling, snatched toys, and the echoing cries of "He/She started it!" It's a near-universal experience for parents of multiple children, a tempest in a teacup that can quickly escalate into a full-blown hurricane of resentment and

conflict. But before you despair, understand this: sibling rivalry, while undeniably challenging, is also a completely normal part of childhood development. It's a testament to the complex emotional landscape of growing up, a process of learning to navigate relationships, negotiate boundaries, and understand the concept of sharing – not just material possessions, but parental attention and love.

The intensity of sibling rivalry varies greatly depending on factors like age differences, personalities, and the family dynamic. A significant age gap can sometimes lessen the intensity of competition, as older siblings may view their younger counterparts with a mixture of protectiveness and exasperation, rather than direct rivalry. However, even with large age gaps, competition can emerge over parental attention and approval. Conversely, children closer in age may find themselves locked in a constant battle for

dominance, mirroring each other's actions and seeking to one-up each other at every opportunity.

Personality plays a crucial role too. Two introverted children might exhibit passive-aggressive forms of rivalry, silently vying for their parent's favor through subtle acts of
compliance or defiance. Two extroverted children, on the other hand, might engage in more overt displays of conflict, openly competing for attention and resources. The family dynamic also creates a fertile ground for sibling rivalry to
flourish or wither. Parents who consistently compare
siblings, whether intentionally or unintentionally, often exacerbate existing tensions. Favoritism, even subtle and unconscious favoritism, can leave the less-favored child feeling neglected, resentful, and deeply insecure. Similarly, parents who are overly critical or punitive can inadvertently fuel competition between siblings, creating an atmosphere of fear and distrust.

Understanding the underlying causes of sibling rivalry is the first step towards effective management. Children often fight for a variety of reasons, ranging from the obvious – vying for toys or parental attention – to the less apparent – vying for security, feeling less important or unloved. For example, a child might act out not because they crave more toys but because they feel overshadowed by their sibling's accomplishments or because they see their sibling receiving more time and attention from parents.

Teaching children effective conflict-resolution skills is paramount. This isn't about silencing disagreements; it's about providing them with the tools to navigate conflict constructively. Start by helping them identify their feelings. Encourage them to use "I" statements rather than accusatory ones. Instead of saying, "He took my toy!", guide them to express their feelings as, "I feel upset because my toy was taken without my permission." This subtle shift in language fosters empathy and reduces the defensiveness that often fuels conflict.

Then, teach them active listening skills. Encourage them to listen attentively to their sibling's perspective, even if they don't agree with it. This is a crucial skill in any relationship, and it's particularly important in sibling dynamics. Often, simply acknowledging the other person's feelings can de-escalate a conflict. You can guide this process by asking

questions like, "How do you think your brother feels about this?" or, "Can you try to see things from your sister's point of view?"

Mediation is another valuable tool. Instead of immediately jumping in and dictating a solution, try to guide them

towards finding a compromise. Ask them questions like, "How can you both solve this problem?" or, "What ideas do you have for sharing?" This approach empowers them to take ownership of the conflict resolution process, fostering independence and self-reliance. If mediation fails, however, and the situation escalates, it's important for parents to step in and establish clear consequences for unacceptable behavior.

But conflict resolution isn't just about extinguishing disputes; it's about creating an environment where cooperation thrives. Involve them in collaborative activities, such as baking, gardening, or playing board games that require teamwork. These activities teach them the value of working together towards a common goal, strengthening their bond and fostering a sense of shared accomplishment. Furthermore, fostering a sense of shared responsibility for household chores can teach them teamwork, helping them understand they are part of a team. This can help eliminate a power struggle over who has to do which chores. Encourage them to help each other with tasks, even if it's something as simple as cleaning up after a playtime or helping with a sibling's homework.

Beyond conflict resolution and cooperation, it's crucial to nurture each child's sense of individuality and self-worth.

Make an effort to spend individual quality time with each child, even if it's just for a few minutes each day. Engage in activities they enjoy, listen attentively to their concerns, and show genuine interest in their unique passions and perspectives. This dedicated one-on-one time ensures each child feels seen, heard, and valued, reducing the need to compete for parental attention.

Celebrate their individual accomplishments, however small.

Refrain from constantly comparing them to each other. Focus on their individual strengths and achievements rather than pitting them against each other. Public praise can also be a great way to build each child's self-esteem without making the other feel inadequate. For example, praising one child for their art while praising the other for their kindness or athleticism avoids setting up a competition. This demonstrates a valuing of each individual's unique contributions to the family unit.

Remember that siblings are not merely rivals; they are also potential lifelong friends and confidants. By fostering cooperation, understanding, and individual appreciation, you are cultivating a strong foundation for positive sibling relationships. It's a long-term investment that will pay dividends throughout their lives. The goal isn't to eliminate conflict altogether – that's unrealistic – but to equip them with the emotional intelligence and conflict-resolution skills to navigate disagreements constructively and build a strong, supportive bond.

It's important to address the potential for underlying issues. Sometimes, sibling rivalry masks deeper anxieties or unmet needs. A child who is consistently bullied or feeling neglected may express this through conflict with their siblings. A change in family dynamics – such as the arrival of a new baby or a divorce – can also trigger increased sibling rivalry. In such cases, professional help may be necessary. A therapist can help identify the root causes of the conflict and develop strategies to address them effectively.

Remember, you're not alone in this. Most families experience sibling rivalry at some point. Don't hesitate to reach out to other parents, family members, friends, or professionals for support and advice. Sharing experiences and learning from others can offer valuable perspective and reassurance. Online forums and support groups dedicated to parenting can be helpful resources for connecting with other families facing similar challenges. These platforms provide a space to share experiences, exchange advice, and offer

mutual support. Knowing you're not the only one dealing with these issues can alleviate feelings of isolation and

inadequacy.

Finally, remember to maintain perspective. While sibling rivalry can be intensely frustrating, it's also a valuable

learning opportunity for both parents and children. It's a chance to learn about communication, conflict resolution, and empathy. It's a chance to teach your children valuable life skills that will serve them well beyond their childhood years. The goal is not to achieve perfect harmony but to create a home environment where children feel secure,

loved, and supported, even amidst the inevitable squabbles and disagreements. Celebrate the small victories,

acknowledge their efforts to cooperate, and remember that even the most challenging sibling dynamics can evolve into positive and mutually supportive relationships with patience, understanding, and consistent effort.

The path towards fostering cooperation and understanding between siblings is not a straight line; it's a winding road with bumps, detours, and the occasional unexpected

breakdown. There will be moments when you feel

overwhelmed, frustrated, and ready to throw in the towel. But remember the long-term goal – to equip your children with the skills and emotional intelligence to navigate their relationships effectively and build lasting bonds with each

other. Embrace the journey, celebrate the successes, learn from the setbacks, and above all, remember that you are not alone in this intricate and often challenging dance of sibling relationships. Your patience, understanding, and consistent efforts will pave the way for a future where your children can not only coexist peacefully but also thrive together as a family unit.

26

Setting Clear Limits and Expectations

The transition from the comforting rituals of bedtime to the unpredictable terrain of daily life often brings a new set of challenges. While the gentle lullaby of sleep may have finally lulled your little one into slumber, the day ahead holds the potential for a different kind of battle: the battle of wills that often manifests as defiance and opposition. This isn't about a child being inherently "bad"; it's about a child navigating the complexities of their emotions, their burgeoning sense of independence, and the ever-shifting landscape of their developing world. Understanding this nuance is crucial to responding effectively.

Defiance, in its purest form, is a child's assertion of autonomy. It's a declaration, often unspoken, of "I am my own person, and I have my own thoughts and feelings." While this striving for independence is a vital part of healthy development, it can manifest in ways that are frustrating, even infuriating, to parents. The tantrums, the refusals, the outright disobedience – these are the outward expressions of a child grappling with the internal struggle to balance their desires with the expectations placed upon them.

The key to navigating this turbulent phase lies in striking a delicate balance: setting clear and consistent limits while simultaneously validating your child's feelings and fostering a sense of connection.

This isn't about authoritarian control; it's about guiding your child towards self-regulation and responsible behavior. Think of it as providing a secure
harbor in a stormy sea, offering a sense of safety and
stability while simultaneously allowing your child to explore their own capabilities and develop their resilience.

One of the most effective strategies is proactive limit-setting. This means establishing clear expectations well in advance, rather than reacting in the heat of the moment. Instead of simply saying "No," explain the reasoning behind your rules. For example, instead of forbidding your child from playing with the expensive vase, explain that it's fragile and could break, emphasizing the potential consequences – not just the punishment, but the loss of the object itself. This approach fosters understanding and encourages your child to internalize the rules, rather than simply obeying out of fear of punishment.

Consistency is equally crucial. Once you've established a rule, stick to it. Inconsistency sends mixed signals, creating confusion and undermining your authority. If you tell your child they can't have dessert unless they eat their vegetables, then follow through. Don't give in to whining or pleading; maintain a firm but gentle stance. This consistency builds trust and predictability, creating a sense of security for your child. They need to know they can rely on your guidance, even when they don't agree with it.

When defiance does occur, remember to validate your child's feelings before addressing the behavior. Listen actively to their complaints, empathize with their frustration, and
acknowledge their perspective, even if you don't agree with it. Saying something like, "I can see you're really upset that you can't have another cookie," acknowledges their feelings without condoning the behavior. This approach helps de-escalate the situation and creates a space for open
communication.

Once you've acknowledged their feelings, clearly state the consequences of their behavior. Consequences should be logical and age-appropriate. For instance, if your child refuses to clean their room, the consequence might be a

temporary loss of screen time. The key is to make the consequence directly related to the misbehavior. Avoid using punishments that are emotionally damaging or excessively harsh; the goal is to guide, not to inflict pain.

Maintaining a supportive and loving relationship is crucial throughout this process. Even when your child is being defiant, remember to communicate your love and affection. Physical touch, such as a hug or a reassuring pat on the back, can be incredibly effective in de-escalating tense situations.

Verbal affirmations of your love and support can also help your child feel secure and connected. Remember, the goal isn't to win a battle of wills; it's to nurture a strong and healthy relationship built on mutual respect and

understanding.

Addressing defiance and opposition requires patience, consistency, and a deep understanding of child development.

It's a process, not a quick fix. There will be setbacks, and there will be moments when you feel overwhelmed. But by focusing on clear expectations, consistent consequences, and a nurturing approach, you can guide your child towards greater self-regulation and a stronger parent-child bond.

Consider the example of a six-year-old named Lily who consistently refuses to put away her toys. Instead of

immediately resorting to punishment, her parents could sit down with her and explain the importance of keeping her room tidy. They could highlight the benefits, such as having more space to play and the ease of finding her favorite toys.

They could also involve her in the process, making it a collaborative effort rather than a chore. If she continues to refuse, a logical consequence might be limiting her screen time until her room is cleaned. However, they also make sure to spend some quality time with her later in the day,

demonstrating their love and support even after the discipline.

Another example involves eight-year-old Tom, who constantly argues with his parents. His parents have identified that much of his argumentative behavior stems from his difficulty in expressing his feelings. They work with him on developing his communication skills,

encouraging him to use "I" statements to express his needs and frustrations. When he does argue, they listen patiently to his perspective, validating his feelings even if they don't agree with his behavior. They set clear boundaries,

explaining that arguing is unacceptable, but they also offer him alternative ways to express his anger or frustration. This might involve taking a break, drawing his feelings, or talking to a trusted adult.

These examples highlight the importance of tailoring your approach to your child's individual needs and developmental stage. What works for one child might not work for another.

The key is to be flexible, adaptable, and consistent in your approach. Observe your child's behavior, identify the underlying causes of their defiance, and adjust your strategies accordingly.

Remember, defiance is often a reflection of a child's emotional state, their developmental stage, or their environment. A child struggling with anxiety or depression might exhibit defiance as a coping mechanism. A child who feels unheard or misunderstood might act out as a way to gain attention. Understanding the root cause of the behavior is crucial in developing an effective response.

Moreover, consider the context of the defiance. Is your child consistently defiant, or is it triggered by specific situations?

Does the behavior increase when they're tired, hungry, or

stressed? Identifying these triggers can help you anticipate and mitigate challenging situations. For instance, if your child is particularly prone to defiance after school, you might implement a calming routine that includes a snack, some quiet time, or a specific activity to help them unwind.

It's also important to consider your own parenting style. Are you overly permissive or overly strict? Are you consistent in your expectations and consequences? Reflecting on your own parenting approach can help you identify areas for improvement and create a more supportive and consistent environment for your child. Seek professional guidance if you're struggling to manage your child's defiance. A child psychologist or therapist can provide valuable insights and support, helping you develop effective strategies and address any underlying issues that may be contributing to the
behavior.

Finally, remember that you are not alone. Many parents struggle with defiance and opposition at some point. Connect with other parents, share your experiences, and learn from their insights. Support groups, online forums, and parenting classes can offer valuable resources and a sense of
community. Raising children is a challenging but rewarding journey, and seeking support is a sign of strength, not
weakness. Embrace the challenges, celebrate the victories, and remember that your love and patience are the most
powerful tools you have in guiding your child through the tumultuous waters of adolescence and beyond. The path may be winding, but with consistent effort and unwavering love, you will navigate it successfully, forging a strong and
enduring bond with your child.

27

Supporting Your Child Through Challenges

The echoes of laughter and the comforting rhythm of family life can be abruptly silenced by the unexpected storms of life. Illness, divorce, financial hardship – these are not merely abstract concepts; they are harsh realities that can shatter the fragile equilibrium of a family and leave children feeling lost and vulnerable. As parents, our instinct is to shield our children from pain, to create a bubble of unwavering happiness. But life, in its unpredictable nature, often bursts that bubble. The key, then, is not to prevent the storms, but to equip our children with the tools to weather them.

When illness strikes, whether it's a minor ailment or a serious condition, the impact extends far beyond the physical. A child experiencing pain, discomfort, or fear will naturally express these emotions. Their anxieties may manifest as clinginess, irritability, or regression to earlier behaviors. It's crucial to validate these feelings. Don't dismiss their fears as "silly" or tell them to "be brave." Instead, acknowledge their experience. Say things like, "I know you're feeling scared right now, and that's okay. It's normal to feel scared when you're not feeling well." Offer comfort, reassurance, and age-appropriate explanations about their illness. Involving them in the process of getting better, as much as possible, can also empower them. This could involve letting them choose a special blanket for the couch, allowing them to participate in medication routines (within safe limits, of course), or even giving them a small task related to their recovery, like choosing a favorite movie to watch. Remember, your child isn't just battling an illness; they're battling the emotional turmoil that accompanies it.

Divorce, a particularly jarring experience, can leave children feeling confused, abandoned, and insecure. Their sense of stability is shaken, and their world is suddenly redefined.

The need for open and honest communication becomes paramount. Avoid speaking negatively about the other parent in front of the child; this can sow seeds of resentment and confusion. Instead, focus on reassuring them that both

parents still love them and will continue to be involved in their lives. Establish clear routines and consistent boundaries to provide a sense of normalcy. Consider family counseling, a safe space where children can express their feelings

without judgment and learn healthy coping mechanisms. Remember, children often interpret divorce as a reflection of their own worth, so reinforcing their value and importance is crucial. Spend quality time with your child, engaging in activities they enjoy, and creating new positive memories to help them rebuild their sense of security.

Financial hardship presents its own set of unique challenges.

Children may be sensitive to changes in family dynamics, such as reduced outings, changes in their schooling, or a move to a less affluent neighborhood. They may not fully understand the complexities of financial struggles, but they can certainly sense the tension and anxiety it creates. Openly communicate with your children, adapting your explanation to their age and understanding. Instead of shielding them completely, involving them in age-appropriate ways can foster resilience. This could involve discussing family

budgeting basics, explaining the need for certain sacrifices, and brainstorming cost-saving solutions together. Emphasize that while circumstances may be challenging, family unity and love remain constant. Look for resources in your community, such as food banks, affordable healthcare options, and support programs for families facing financial difficulties. Remember that resilience is not about denying hardship; it's about facing it head-on as a united family.

Beyond these major life events, smaller, seemingly insignificant daily struggles can also impact a child's well-being. The death of a pet, the pressures of school, bullying, or even social anxieties can leave children feeling overwhelmed and vulnerable. It's important to validate their feelings, even if you don't fully understand their perspective. Create a safe space where they feel comfortable expressing themselves without fear of judgment or ridicule. Active listening, where you truly hear and understand their feelings, is more powerful than any lecture or reprimand. Ask open-ended questions, encouraging them to articulate their thoughts and emotions. Help them to problem-solve, offering suggestions and empowering them to find their own solutions. Encourage them to build healthy coping mechanisms, such as engaging in physical activity, pursuing hobbies, or spending time in nature.

Remember that children's resilience isn't inherent; it's nurtured. Your role as a parent is not to eliminate challenges but to provide the scaffolding of support, empathy, and understanding that allows them to navigate the rough patches. The strength of your bond, the security of your love, and the unwavering support you offer will be the most valuable tools they have in facing any storm life throws their way. This isn't about shielding them from hardship; it's about equipping them with the emotional armor to confront it, learn from it, and emerge stronger.

The process of navigating difficult times with children is not a linear one; it's a journey filled with twists, turns, and unexpected detours. There will be days when you feel overwhelmed, frustrated, and even inadequate. This is normal. Allow yourself to feel these emotions without judgment. Seek support from your partner, friends, family, or professionals. Parenting support groups, therapy sessions, or even casual conversations with other parents can offer invaluable insights and a sense of community. Remember, asking for help is not a sign of weakness; it's a testament to your strength and commitment to your child's well-being.

One often overlooked aspect is the importance of self-care for the parent. You cannot pour from an empty cup. When you are feeling depleted, stressed, or overwhelmed, your capacity to provide support for your child diminishes significantly. Prioritize self-care activities, even if it means just a few minutes each day. Engage in activities that bring you joy, relaxation, or a sense of peace. This could be anything from reading a book, taking a walk in nature, listening to music, or spending time with supportive friends.

Remember, taking care of yourself is not selfish; it's a necessity for being the best parent you can be. Your well-being directly impacts your child's well-being.

Furthermore, it's crucial to tailor your approach to your child's unique personality and developmental stage. A toddler will react differently to a stressful situation than a teenager. Younger children may express their distress through tantrums, clinginess, or regression, whereas older children might withdraw, become irritable, or exhibit changes in their behavior or school performance.

Understanding your child's individual coping mechanisms and emotional cues is essential for providing effective support.

Finally, fostering a sense of hope and optimism is vital.

While acknowledging the challenges and validating your child's emotions, it's equally important to emphasize the positive aspects of the situation and focus on the future. Help your child identify their strengths and resilience, and

encourage them to set realistic goals and celebrate their achievements, no matter how small. Remind them that even

in the darkest times, there is always a light at the end of the tunnel. This sense of hope will empower them to navigate difficult times with increased confidence and resilience.

Remember, the challenges you face as a parent are not a measure of your success or failure; they are an integral part of the parenting journey. By equipping yourself with the knowledge and strategies to support your child through difficult times, you can foster their emotional well-being and create a resilient, loving, and supportive family unit that can weather any storm. And through that shared journey, you'll not only help your child grow stronger but also discover a strength within yourself that you never knew you possessed.

<h1 style="text-align:center">28</h1>

Creating Meaningful Shared Experiences

Family time isn't just about ticking off items on a to-do list; it's the lifeblood of a strong family unit. It's the glue that binds you together, creating a shared history filled with laughter, learning, and love. In the whirlwind of daily

routines, it's easy to lose sight of the importance of dedicated family time, but investing in these moments is an investment in the future happiness and well-being of your family.

Remember, children thrive on connection, and consistent quality time provides the fertile ground for emotional growth, resilience, and a deep sense of belonging.

Think back to your own childhood. What are your most cherished memories? Chances are, many of them involve time spent with your family – a weekend camping trip, a boisterous game of charades, a quiet evening reading

together. These weren't necessarily extravagant events; their power lay in the shared experience, the laughter, the

connection. This is precisely what we aim to recreate with our own children. It's about creating a tapestry of shared memories, woven with threads of love, laughter, and

connection.

The key to successful family time isn't about grand gestures or expensive outings; it's about intentionality and presence. It's about being fully present, putting aside distractions like phones and screens, and genuinely engaging with your
children. It's about creating a space where they feel seen, heard, and valued. This might involve a simple game of catch in the backyard, baking cookies together, or even just cuddling up on the couch to read a book. The activity itself is secondary; the focus is on the interaction, the connection, and the shared experience.

One effective strategy is to establish regular family rituals.

This could be a weekly game night, a Sunday morning
breakfast together, or a nightly story time before bed. These rituals create a sense of predictability and stability, providing a consistent anchor in the sometimes chaotic world of family life. They also offer a predictable and enjoyable time for bonding and connection. The consistency reinforces the importance of family time and creates a sense of anticipation and excitement for these special moments.

Beyond regular rituals, incorporating spontaneous acts of connection is equally crucial. This could involve a surprise picnic in the park, a spontaneous dance party in the living room, or even just a few minutes of focused one-on-one time with each child. These spontaneous moments often hold a special magic, fostering a sense of fun and unpredictability that strengthens the bond between parents and children. They show children that family time is valued and that their parents are invested in their happiness.

Consider the different developmental stages of your children when planning family activities. What engages a toddler might bore a teenager. For younger children, simple
activities that focus on sensory exploration, such as playing with playdough, painting, or building a sandcastle, can be incredibly enriching. These activities stimulate their
imaginations, foster creativity, and provide opportunities for you to engage with them in their world. With older children, you might en-

gage in board games, card games, or even collaborative projects like building a birdhouse or painting a mural.

Incorporate a variety of activities to cater to every family member's interests. This could range from watching a movie together to going for a hike in the woods, from cooking a

meal as a team to playing a family board game. The goal is to find activities that everyone enjoys and that foster a sense of shared accomplishment. Diversity in activities ensures that family time doesn't become monotonous and that

everyone feels valued and included in the process of

selecting activities.

Don't underestimate the power of simple conversations.

During family time, encourage open communication. Ask your children about their day, their friends, their interests, and their feelings. Listen actively to their responses, showing genuine interest and empathy. These conversations are not just about gathering information; they're about deepening your understanding of your children, nurturing your

relationships, and creating a space where they feel

comfortable sharing their thoughts and feelings.

Make technology a tool, not a barrier. While it's essential to minimize screen time during family time, technology can be a valuable resource when used intentionally. For example, you could use a family-friendly app to play games together, watch a nature documentary that sparks conversation, or even use video chat to connect with distant family members.

The key is to use technology mindfully, ensuring that it enhances your family time rather than detracting from it.

Remember that family time isn't always about extravagant events or elaborate activities. Sometimes, the most

meaningful moments are the simplest ones. A quiet evening reading together, a walk in the park, or even just cuddling on the couch can create lasting memories and strengthen your family bond. These seemingly small moments are often the ones that children remember most fondly, and they form the cornerstone of a strong and loving family relationship.

Family meals are a powerful opportunity for connection. They are a time to share stories, discuss the day's events, and simply enjoy each other's company. Try to make mealtimes a phone-free zone, creating a space for conversation and

connection. Involve your children in meal preparation –whether it's setting the table, washing vegetables, or even helping to cook a simple dish. This shared experience not only teaches them valuable life skills but also strengthens family bonds.

Incorporate family vacations or weekend getaways into your family time plan. These trips don't have to be extravagant; even a simple camping trip in the backyard or a day trip to a nearby park can create lasting memories and strengthen family bonds. These experiences provide opportunities for shared adventures, creating a sense of camaraderie and shared purpose. The focus should be on creating shared experiences and making memories together, rather than on the destination itself.

Don't be afraid to experiment with different activities and find what works best for your family. There's no one-size-fits-all approach to family time. The key is to find activities that everyone enjoys and that promote connection and

bonding. Be flexible, be creative, and most importantly, be present. Remember that the most valuable investment you can make is in your family relationships. These connections will shape the lives of your children, nurturing their growth, resilience, and overall well-being. By investing in

meaningful family time, you're not just creating memories; you're creating a legacy of love and connection that will last a lifetime. The laughter, the shared experiences, the feeling of belonging – these are the treasures that will enrich your family's life immeasurably. And as your children grow, the memories you create together will form the foundation of their self-esteem and their ability to form healthy

relationships in the future. So make time, make memories, and make your family time count. The investment you make today will yield invaluable dividends for years to come.

29

Recognizing and Rewarding Efforts

Building upon the foundation of consistent quality time and shared experiences, we now move to a crucial element in fostering a strong and lasting bond with your child:
celebrating their achievements. It's not merely about the trophies and accolades; it's about acknowledging the
journey, the effort, the perseverance, and the small victories along the way. These celebrations are the building blocks of self-esteem and confidence, laying the groundwork for future success and resilience.

Think back to your own childhood. Do you remember a time when a seemingly small accomplishment was met with genuine enthusiasm and praise from a parent or loved one? The feeling of pride and validation, that sense of being seen and appreciated, likely left a lasting impression. This isn't just about nostalgia; it's a powerful illustration of the
profound impact of positive reinforcement on a child's
development.

Celebrating achievements isn't about showering your child with material rewards every time they accomplish
something. It's about creating a culture of acknowledgment and appreciation within your family. It's about fostering a deeper connection through shared joy and pride. The focus should be on the process, the

effort, the resilience, and the lessons learned, as much as on the outcome itself. A child who learns to value the journey will develop a growth mindset—a belief that abilities and intelligence can be developed through dedication and hard work—rather than a fixed mindset, which limits their potential.

Consider a child learning to ride a bicycle. The initial wobbles, the falls, the scraped knees – these are all part of the process. While the ultimate goal is riding independently, the celebrations should begin much earlier. Celebrate their courage in attempting to balance, their persistence in getting back on after a fall, and their gradual improvement in coordination and confidence. Each small step forward deserves recognition and praise. "Wow, you're getting so much better at balancing! I can see how hard you're working." This approach, focusing on the effort rather than solely on the result, builds resilience and a positive attitude towards challenges.

This principle extends far beyond physical activities.

Academic achievements, artistic endeavors, acts of kindness, overcoming personal challenges – all these warrant recognition and celebration. When your child receives a good grade on a test, avoid simply saying, "Good job." Instead, delve deeper: "I noticed you studied really hard for this test. I'm proud of your dedication and how you organized your time." Similarly, if your child demonstrates empathy towards a friend in need, acknowledge their compassion: "I saw how you helped your friend. That was incredibly kind and thoughtful of you."

The method of celebration should be tailored to your child's personality and preferences. For some, a simple hug and words of affirmation may suffice. For others, a small, meaningful gift or a special outing might be more effective.

The key is to make the celebration genuine and heartfelt, reflecting the unique bond you share with your child.

Avoid comparing your child's achievements to those of siblings or peers. Each child is unique, with their own strengths and weaknesses, their own pace of development.

Comparisons can foster feelings of inadequacy and resentment, undermining their sense of self-worth. Instead, focus on their individual progress and celebrate their personal triumphs. Remember, the goal isn't to foster competition, but to nurture their self-belief and confidence.

Incorporating regular family meetings can provide a structured opportunity for celebrating achievements. During these meetings, each family member can share their successes, big or small, fostering a sense of unity and shared pride. This can be as simple as a casual dinner conversation or a more formal gathering, depending on your family's dynamic. The crucial element is creating a space where everyone feels comfortable sharing their experiences and receiving positive feedback.

Remember, the impact of celebrating achievements extends far beyond immediate gratification. It fosters a positive self-image, resilience in the face of setbacks, and a sense of self-efficacy – the belief in one's ability to succeed. Children who feel seen, heard, and appreciated are more likely to be motivated to strive for excellence, embrace challenges, and develop a lifelong love of learning. This approach instills a deep-seated sense of self-worth, empowering them to navigate the complexities of life with confidence and grace.

Let's explore some specific examples to illuminate these principles. Imagine your eight-year-old daughter, Lily, has been struggling with learning her multiplication tables.

Instead of focusing solely on the correct answers, acknowledge her effort and persistence. "Lily, I know you've been working really hard on your multiplication tables. I've noticed how much time you've dedicated to practicing, and I'm so proud of your perseverance. Even though some days were tougher than others, you kept trying, and that's what matters most." You could then offer a small reward, like a

special movie night or a trip to the ice cream parlor, not as a bribe, but as a way to share in her accomplishment.

Or consider your teenage son, Tom, who recently overcame his fear of public speaking by presenting a project to his class. This requires a different approach than celebrating a perfect math score. "Tom, I was so impressed with your courage in presenting your project today. I know how

nervous you were, but you faced your fear head-on and delivered an amazing presentation. That takes real strength and bravery." In this instance, a reward might be a quiet evening of his choice, acknowledging the emotional effort involved.

The key is to make the celebration specific and genuine.

Avoid generic praise like "Good job" or "That's great." Instead, highlight the specific efforts and qualities you admire. Notice the small details, the perseverance, the effort put forth, the strategies employed. This level of attention communicates your love, respect, and understanding in a powerful way.

In addition to celebrating individual achievements, don't forget to celebrate family accomplishments. Reaching a shared goal, completing a family project, or simply

navigating a challenging situation together deserves

recognition. These shared victories further strengthen the family bond and create lasting memories. Perhaps it's the successful completion of a family garden, the planning and execution of a family vacation, or overcoming a financial hardship as a united front. These shared experiences forge stronger bonds and build resilience within the family unit.

Moreover, consider incorporating acts of service as a way to celebrate achievements. After your child achieves a

significant milestone, encourage them to perform a kind act

for someone else. This fosters a sense of empathy and community, further enriching their sense of accomplishment and reinforcing positive values. It's not just about recognizing individual success; it's about fostering a sense of responsibility and contribution to the wider community.

The ultimate goal of celebrating achievements isn't simply to reward your child for their accomplishments, but to cultivate a deep and lasting connection built on mutual respect, understanding, and shared joy. By consistently acknowledging their efforts and celebrating their successes, both big and small, you're investing in their self-esteem, resilience, and overall well-being, laying a solid foundation for a happy and fulfilling life. This consistent affirmation is more than just praise; it's the fuel that powers their future endeavors and solidifies the strong bond you share.

Remember, these moments of shared celebration are the threads that weave the rich tapestry of your family's enduring connection. They're the memories that will be cherished for a lifetime.

30

Showing Your Love Through Actions

Beyond the words of praise and the shared laughter of celebration lies another powerful avenue for strengthening your bond with your child: acts of service. These aren't grand gestures, but rather small, consistent demonstrations of love and care that speak volumes louder than any declaration.

They are the quiet acts of kindness that weave themselves into the fabric of your family life, creating a tapestry of affection and mutual respect. Think of it as a silent language of love, understood not through words but through meaningful actions.

For young children, acts of service might take the form of simple, everyday tasks. Helping them build a magnificent block tower, even if it inevitably collapses in a joyful avalanche, is a demonstration of your willingness to participate in their world. Reading them a bedtime story, not just as a routine, but with genuine engagement and enthusiasm, creating a cozy, intimate moment of connection.

Preparing their favorite meal, taking extra care in presentation, turning a simple dinner into a small celebration. These are moments that build a sense of security and belonging, telling your child, without words, "I care for you, I see you, and I am here for you."

As children grow older, the acts of service evolve, mirroring their increasing independence and their developing sense of responsibility. Helping with chores, not as a choreographed task, but as a shared effort, fostering a sense of collaboration and teamwork within the family dynamic. Offering

assistance with homework, not as a means of taking over, but as a guiding hand, encouraging their problem-solving skills and fostering their self-reliance. Driving them to practices

and appointments, not merely as a transportation service, but as a moment of shared conversation and connection,

listening to their stories and engaging in their world. These acts are not just about completing tasks; they are about building a stronger connection and showing your child that their needs and pursuits are important to you.

The key to effective acts of service lies in intentionality and authenticity. It's about setting aside distractions, putting down your phone, and truly engaging with your child in the moment. It's about making eye contact, offering a genuine smile, and listening attentively to what they have to say, creating a space for them to feel seen and heard. This is not simply about doing something for them; it's about showing that you're actively participating in their lives and sharing in their experiences, big and small.

Consider the teenager who struggles with managing their time and organization. Instead of lecturing, offer practical help, like creating a shared family calendar or assisting them in developing a more efficient study schedule. This

demonstrates support and understanding, showing that you care about their success, not just their grades. Or perhaps your teenager is consumed by the anxieties of social media.

Instead of criticism, create opportunities for meaningful conversations, engaging in activities that promote face-to-face interaction and fostering a stronger sense of connection and belonging. This builds trust and rapport, a necessary foundation for open communication and mutual support.

For adolescents grappling with the complexities of self-identity and independence, acts of service can take a

different form. Listening to their anxieties and frustrations without judgment, offering a supportive ear, and validating their feelings. Respecting their individuality and allowing them space to express themselves freely and openly, even if

it means disagreeing. Supporting their passions and interests, even if they differ greatly from your own, demonstrating your unconditional love and acceptance. These acts of

empathy and understanding are far more valuable than any material gift, fostering a sense of trust and respect that lays the groundwork for a lasting and meaningful relationship.

The beauty of acts of service lies in their adaptability. They can be tailored to your child's specific needs, interests, and developmental stage, making them a uniquely effective tool for nurturing connection. A child who loves to bake might find joy in helping you prepare cookies or a cake, turning the chore into a shared experience of creativity and

collaboration. A child who enjoys gardening can assist in planting flowers or tending the vegetable patch, fostering a connection with nature and nurturing responsibility. These activities not only strengthen your bond but also teach

valuable life skills and foster a sense of accomplishment.

Think beyond the immediate tasks. Acts of service can also encompass larger gestures of love and support. Helping your child overcome a fear, supporting them through a difficult challenge, offering encouragement during a time of struggle.

These are demonstrations of your unwavering support and belief in their abilities. They demonstrate that you're not only there for the easy moments but also for the tough ones, reaffirming your commitment to your child's well-being, no matter what life throws their way.

Remember, acts of service are not transactional; they are not about earning gratitude or expecting repayment. They are expressions of genuine love and affection, intended to
nourish the bond you share with your child. The goal is to create a climate of mutual respect, where both parent and child feel seen, heard, and valued. It's about fostering a family culture where kindness and consideration are the
norm, where everyone feels safe to be themselves and to express their needs and concerns without fear of judgment.

In essence, acts of service are not about grand displays of affection; they are about the quiet, consistent, and loving actions that speak volumes about the depth of your
connection. It is in these seemingly small moments, in the shared chores, the supportive words, and the attentive
listening, that the foundation of a strong and lasting family bond is truly built. They are the unspoken pledges of love, the silent promises that affirm your commitment to your child's well-being and the enduring strength of your family connection. These seemingly small acts accumulate,
becoming significant milestones in your child's life,
representing a testament to the powerful bond you have painstakingly cultivated. They are the quiet whispers of love that echo through the years, shaping the individual your child grows into, creating lasting memories, and fostering a relationship that will endure for a lifetime. Embrace these acts of service, not as tasks, but as opportunities to deepen your connection, to nurture your child's growth, and to cultivate a family bond that will withstand the test of time.

31

Expressing Your Love and Appreciation

Words, potent tools of connection, often hold more weight than grand gestures. They are the building blocks of emotional intimacy, the threads that weave together a tapestry of love and understanding within the family. While acts of service demonstrate love through action, words of affirmation express it directly, validating your child's worth and strengthening their self-esteem. These aren't empty platitudes; they are carefully chosen phrases that resonate deeply, acknowledging their efforts, celebrating their achievements, and bolstering their confidence during challenging times. The power of these affirmations lies not just in the words themselves, but in the genuine affection and sincerity with which they are delivered.

Think of it as a daily ritual of love, a quiet affirmation of your child's inherent value. It's in the casual "I love you," whispered before bedtime, or the heartfelt "I'm so proud of you," offered after a difficult school presentation. It's the spontaneous "You make me so happy," shared during a moment of shared joy, or the comforting "I'm here for you, no matter what," offered during a time of distress. These seemingly simple statements are powerful tools that build resilience and foster a strong sense of self-worth in your child.

The key is consistency. Regular affirmations, woven into the fabric of your daily interactions, create a climate of love and acceptance that permeates your home. It's not about
showering your child with excessive praise for every minor accomplishment; it's about recognizing genuine effort, celebrating milestones, both big and small, and offering unwavering support during setbacks. The goal is to create a
secure base from which your child can explore their potential, knowing they are unconditionally loved and cherished.

Consider the impact of specific phrases tailored to your child's unique personality and current developmental stage.

A young child might respond well to simple affirmations like, "You're such a good helper," or "I love how kind you are to your little brother." For an older child, more
sophisticated affirmations might be more appropriate, such as, "I'm impressed by your perseverance on that project," or "I admire your creativity and dedication." The key is to be specific and genuine, focusing on observable behaviors and traits rather than offering generic praise. Instead of saying "You're smart," try, "I'm amazed by how quickly you solved that math problem." The former is vague and potentially hollow; the latter is specific, highlighting a concrete accomplishment and fostering a growth mindset.

This approach also allows you to address specific challenges your child might be facing. If your child is struggling with a particular subject in school, instead of simply saying "You can do it," try a more supportive approach such as, "I know this is tough, but I see how hard you're working, and I'm proud of your effort." This acknowledges the difficulty while reinforcing their perseverance. If they are experiencing social difficulties, you might say, "I see how much you care about your friends, and I'm proud of your willingness to reach out and connect with others." This focuses on their positive qualities, even while acknowledging the challenges they face.

Furthermore, words of affirmation extend beyond spoken praise. Written notes, carefully selected gifts that reflect their interests, or even a simple hug can convey your love and appreciation in powerful ways. A short note tucked into their

lunchbox, a small gift reflecting a shared interest, a heartfelt email acknowledging their recent success, these seemingly small gestures are potent reminders of your love and support.

Consider leaving a handwritten note on their pillow, expressing your love and appreciation for their unique qualities. These actions demonstrate your thoughtfulness and create lasting memories.

The impact of these words extends far beyond the present moment. Children who receive consistent affirmations develop a stronger sense of self-worth, resilience, and confidence. They are more likely to approach challenges with optimism, knowing they have a supportive and loving family to rely on. They develop a stronger sense of self-efficacy – the belief in their ability to succeed – which is crucial for their academic, social, and emotional development. Conversely, a lack of positive affirmation can lead to low self-esteem, anxiety, and a reluctance to take risks.

Think about your own childhood. Do you remember specific words or actions from your parents that made you feel loved and appreciated? These memories likely played a significant role in shaping your sense of self and your ability to navigate life's challenges. Now, consider the opportunity you have to create similar positive memories for your own children. By intentionally using words of affirmation, you are actively shaping their self-perception and contributing to their overall well-being.

It's not just about the words themselves, but the context in which they are delivered. Affirmations are most effective when they are genuine, specific, and consistent. Avoid using empty praise or hyperbole; focus instead on sincere recognition of your child's effort, achievements, and positive quali-ties. The tone of your voice also plays a crucial role; a

warm, loving tone will convey sincerity and enhance the impact of your words. Your body language should also reflect your genuine af-fection, whether it's a warm hug, a gentle touch, or a loving smile.

Consider incorporating words of affirmation into your daily rou-tine. Start by taking a few minutes each day to connect with your child, offering specific praise for their behavior or accomplishments. You might say, "I noticed you helped your sister with her homework today – that was incredibly kind and thoughtful," or "I'm so proud of how you handled that challenging situation with grace and maturity." These

specific observations showcase your attention and

demonstrate your appreciation for their positive actions.

Remember, words of affirmation are not a quick fix or a magic solution; they are a consistent, ongoing effort that requires patience, understanding, and commitment.

However, the rewards are immeasurable. By nurturing your child's emotional well-being through the power of positive words, you are building a strong foundation for a lasting and loving family connec-tion. It's a process that requires

consistency and mindfulness, but the investment is well worth the ef-fort. The bond you cultivate will serve as a

lifelong source of strength and support for your child,

shaping their character and influencing their future

interactions with the world. It is, in essence, an investment in their future, a legacy of love and appreciation that will

endure long after the words themselves are spoken.

Furthermore, the power of affirmation extends beyond the imme-diate family unit. By modeling positive communication and express-ing appreciation for others, you are teaching your children valuable social skills and fostering a culture of empathy and respect within

your family and beyond. This creates a positive ripple effect, influencing their interactions
with peers, teachers, and other adults in their lives. It teaches them the importance of building strong, healthy relationships based on mutual respect and appreciation.

The process of actively choosing and expressing these
affirmations is itself a powerful act of love. It requires you to pause, observe, and truly appreciate your child's unique qualities and accomplishments. It's a chance to connect on a deeper emotional level, reinforcing your bond and creating a shared experience of love and appreciation. This mindful approach fosters a sense of closeness and understanding, strengthening the family bond and creating a supportive environment where children feel safe, secure, and cherished.

In conclusion, words of affirmation are not simply words; they are powerful tools for shaping your child's self-
perception and fostering a lasting, loving family connection, a testament to the power of language to build strong family ties. They are the quiet declarations of love that resonate through the years, building a legacy of warmth and
understanding that enriches the lives of both parent and child.

32

Investing in Meaningful Interactions

In the whirlwind of daily life, it's easy to let precious moments slip away unnoticed. The demands of work, school, and household chores can leave us feeling perpetually rushed, our interactions with our children often reduced to hurried goodbyes and fleeting exchanges. But amidst the chaos, it's crucial to remember that the cornerstone of a strong family bond isn't just about quantity of time spent together, but the
quality
of that time. It's about creating space for meaningful interactions, for genuine connection, for the shared experiences that forge lasting memories and deepen your relationship with your child.

Investing in quality time isn't about grand gestures or extravagant vacations. It's about the small, deliberate choices we make every day to prioritize connection. It's about setting aside distractions, turning off the screens, and truly being present with your child. It's about creating a space where they feel safe, seen, and heard, where they know you're fully engaged with them and their world.

Consider the power of a shared bedtime story, read not just for the sake of routine, but as an opportunity to snuggle close, to whisper words of love and affirmation, to build a cozy sanctuary of connection. Imagine the delight in a spontaneous game of catch in the backyard, the laughter echoing through the air, the simple joy of shared physical activity that strengthens both your bond and your bodies. Or perhaps it's the quiet intimacy of baking cookies together, the flour dusting your aprons, the sweet scent filling the air, a shared creation that becomes a symbol of your collaborative spirit.

These seemingly small moments, when infused with intention and presence, become powerful catalysts for connection. They create lasting memories, strengthen family ties, and build a foundation of trust and mutual respect. But carving out this quality time, especially in today's busy world, requires conscious effort and strategic planning.

One effective strategy is to establish dedicated family time, a regular ritual that everyone looks forward to. This could be a weekly game night, a monthly family outing, or even just a half-hour each evening devoted to uninterrupted family conversation. Consistency is key here, establishing a predictable pattern that your child can anticipate and cherish.

The regularity itself fosters a sense of security and belonging, letting your child know they are valued and their time with you is a priority.

However, creating meaningful moments isn't simply about scheduling specific time slots. It's also about weaving connection into the fabric of your daily life. Involve your child in age-appropriate household tasks, turning chores into opportunities for shared learning and bonding. Let them help with meal preparation, teaching them about healthy eating and providing a chance for focused interaction. Assign them small responsibilities, fostering a sense of independence and contribution within the family unit. Even simple acts, like folding laundry together or helping with the gardening, offer moments of connection and shared accomplishment.

Another crucial aspect of quality time is active listening.

This means putting down your phone, making eye contact, and truly focusing on what your child is saying, not just waiting for your turn to speak. Ask open-ended questions that encourage them to elaborate, show genuine interest in their thoughts and feelings, and validate their experiences. Children often express themselves through nonverbal cues as

well; pay close attention to their body language, tone of voice, and facial expressions to understand the deeper meaning behind their words. This active listening fosters a sense of being heard and understood, strengthening their self-esteem and encouraging them to open up to you more readily.

Furthermore, create a space where open communication is encouraged. Establish a safe and non-judgmental

environment where your child feels comfortable sharing their thoughts and feelings, both positive and negative. This doesn't mean you need to agree with everything they say, but it does mean actively listening, validating their emotions, and offering guidance without criticism. Regular family meetings can be helpful in establishing this open dialogue, creating a structured space for sharing concerns, celebrating successes, and making family decisions collaboratively.

These meetings shouldn't feel like interrogations; instead, cultivate a relaxed, supportive atmosphere where everyone feels empowered to participate.

Screen time, while undeniably a part of modern life, can often hinder quality time. Establish clear boundaries on screen usage, ensuring that it doesn't consume the majority of your shared time. Create screen-free zones and times, such as during mealtimes, bedtime, and dedicated family activities. Encourage alternative activities that promote interaction and engagement, such as playing board games, reading together, engaging in creative projects, or exploring nature. These activities foster a sense of shared experience and strengthen your bond while simultaneously teaching valuable life skills.

Remember, quality time isn't about performing elaborate acts; it's about the genuine connection you create through shared experiences. A simple walk in the park, a quiet

evening spent drawing together, a spontaneous dance party in the living room—these seemingly ordinary moments, imbued with attention and affection, become the building blocks of a strong and lasting family bond. The key is to be intentional, to be present, to choose connection over

distraction, and to cultivate a space where your child feels loved, valued, and understood.

Moreover, adapting your approach to your child's age and developmental stage is vital. What resonates with a toddler won't necessarily connect with a teenager. For younger

children, simple playtime, shared reading, and nurturing routines are crucial. As they grow older, meaningful

conversations, shared hobbies, and collaborative projects become increasingly important. Always strive to understand your child's unique interests and tailor your quality time accordingly. This demonstrates respect for their individuality and strengthens your connection on a deeper level.

Sometimes, life throws curveballs. Unexpected events, work pressures, or personal challenges can disrupt our well-laid plans for quality time. When this happens, don't beat

yourself up. Acknowledge the challenges, and strive to find small pockets of connection amidst the chaos. Even a few minutes of focused attention, a heartfelt hug, or a simple "I love you" can make a world of difference. The most

important aspect of quality time is the consistent effort to prioritize your relationship with your child, demonstrating love and understanding through both big and small gestures.

Ultimately, the goal of investing in quality time is to build a strong foundation of trust and mutual respect. It's about fostering a deep emotional connection that will sustain your family through the joys

and challenges of life. It's an
investment that pays dividends far beyond the moments themselves,
shaping your child's emotional well-being, self-

esteem, and overall development. It creates a lasting legacy of
love and connection, a family bond that endures through time. So,
make the conscious decision today to prioritize quality time with your
child. You won't regret it. The
memories you create, the bonds you strengthen, and the love you
share will be invaluable treasures that will enrich your lives for years
to come. Embrace the present, nurture the connection, and watch
your family bond flourish. The
rewards are immeasurable.

33

Acknowledgments

Writing this book has been a journey, and I'm deeply grateful to all those who have supported me along the way. First and foremost, I want to thank my family for their unwavering patience and understanding during the long hours spent researching and writing. Their love and support have been my constant source of inspiration. I am also indebted to the many parents and children I've had the privilege of working with over the years. Your stories, struggles, and triumphs have enriched this book immeasurably and provided the foundation for the practical advice offered within. A special thank you goes to my editor, [Editor's Name], for their

insightful feedback and guidance in shaping this manuscript into its final form. Their expertise and dedication have been invaluable. Finally, I want to express my gratitude to the researchers and professionals whose work has informed my understanding of child development and parenting. Their contributions have been instrumental in creating this

comprehensive guide.

34

Glossary

This glossary provides definitions of key terms used throughout the book to ensure clarity and understanding.

Active Listening:

Paying full attention to a child's communication, both verbal and nonverbal, without interrupting or judging.

Emotional Validation:

Acknowledging and accepting a child's feelings, even if you don't agree with their behavior.

Empathy:

The ability to understand and share the feelings of another person.

Resilience:

The ability to bounce back from adversity and cope with challenges.

Self-Regulation:

The ability to manage one's own emotions and behavior.